Day Trading Kills

A Must-Read for ANYONE Considering Day Trading Forex, Futures, Stocks, Options, and Cryptocurrencies

Second Edition

Ali Roghani

Day Trading Kills: A Must-Read for ANYONE Considering Day Trading Forex, Futures, Stocks, Options, and Cryptocurrencies

This publication is designed to provide accurate and authoritative information regarding the subject matter covered. It is sold with the understanding that neither the author nor the publisher is engaged in rendering legal, investment, accounting, tax, or other professional services. The author has used best efforts in preparing this book; however, no representations or warranties are made with respect to the accuracy or completeness of the contents. Any implied warranties of merchantability or fitness for a particular purpose are specifically disclaimed. The advice and strategies contained herein may not be suitable for your situation. You should consult with a qualified professional when appropriate. Neither the publisher nor the author shall be liable for any loss of profit or any other commercial damages, including but not limited to special, incidental, consequential, personal, or other damages.

Quotations and frameworks attributed to Benjamin Graham and Warren Buffett are paraphrased for instructional purposes; no copyrighted text from *The Intelligent Investor* or from Berkshire Hathaway shareholder letters has been reproduced. Readers are encouraged to consult the original sources directly.

Important Disclaimer

This book is an educational and editorial work about the risks of day trading and the principles of long-term investing. It is not personalized financial, investment, legal, accounting, or tax advice. The author and publisher are not registered investment advisors and do not provide individualized recommendations.

Trading and investing in financial markets involve substantial risk, including the possible loss of principal. Past performance does not guarantee future results. The strategies, examples, and reference numbers in this book are illustrative; they may not be appropriate for your specific objectives, time horizon, tax situation, or risk tolerance.

Regulatory authorities including the U.S. Securities and Exchange Commission and the Financial Industry Regulatory Authority publish materials specifically warning that day trading is extremely risky and that the typical participant experiences substantial financial losses.

Before acting on any idea discussed here, consider consulting a fiduciary financial advisor, a tax professional, and, where relevant, a licensed mental-health professional. Trade names, products, and services mentioned in this book are the property of their respective owners.

Contents

Chapter 1

Introduction

Day trading is the practice of buying and selling financial instruments inside a single day, hoping to profit from short-term price moves. People trade stocks, foreign currencies, futures, options, and cryptocurrencies this way. Trading apps make it easy to start. Online videos make it look exciting. Most of the people who try it lose money.

That is the central message of this book, and it has not changed since the first edition. What has changed is what we know. We have more years of data, more failed accounts, more regulator warnings, and a better picture of how the activity actually plays out for ordinary people. The numbers are not encouraging.

Studies in different countries point in the same direction. A large study of Brazilian futures traders found that almost everyone who kept trading for more than a few hundred days lost money, and only a tiny share earned more than a basic minimum wage. Studies of Taiwanese traders reach a similar conclusion. The U.S. Securities and Exchange Commission and FINRA tell the same story in plainer words on their public investor pages: day trading is risky, most participants lose, and you should not use money you cannot afford to lose.

This is not a gambling book and it is not a get-rich book. It is a warning, written by someone who has watched the harm up close. The first edition focused on the warning. This second edition keeps that focus and adds something the first edition did less of: clear, plain explanations of why the math, the markets, and the human mind work against the day trader. The point is not to scare anyone. The point is to give you enough understanding that, whatever you decide to do, you decide it with eyes open.

What this book covers

The chapters that follow walk through the day-trading world from several angles.

- The methods people use to trade and the markets they trade in.
- How day trading differs from real investing — and what real investing actually looks like.
- What moves prices, and why short-term price moves are so hard to predict.
- The tools traders rely on, including charts and company analysis, and where those tools fall short.
- The role of emotions, leverage, hidden fees, and market manipulation.
- The toll on physical and mental health, on relationships, and on personal stability.
- The traps: addiction, scams, signal sellers, automated bots.
- Better and safer paths for building wealth, drawn from long-tested investing ideas.

What this book is not

This book is not personal financial advice. It does not tell you what stock to buy, what fund to choose, or how to manage your taxes. Your situation is your own. A licensed advisor who knows your full picture can do that work; a book cannot.

It is also not a course. There are no signals to subscribe to, no system to buy, no private group to join. If a book on day trading is selling you something at the end, the book is the bait. This one is not.

How to read it

Read it straight through if you are deciding whether to start. Skip to the chapters on math, leverage, and fees if you are already trading and want to understand your real costs. Go to the chapters on health, family, and addiction if the activity is starting to take more than it gives. Read the final chapter on safer alternatives if you want a calmer way to build wealth over time. The book is short enough to finish in a few sittings and detailed enough to come back to.

One last note before we begin. Nothing here is meant to mock anyone who has tried day trading and lost. Most people who get pulled in are smart, motivated, and looking for a way out of a system that does not feel like it is working for them. The motive is good. The method, on the evidence, is not. The point of the next two hundred pages is to make that case clearly enough that the next decision you make is a better one.

A note on the data

When this book quotes a number, it points to the source. Readers who want to verify any specific claim can do so in a few clicks. The most important sources used throughout are public regulatory pages from the U.S. Securities and Exchange Commission and FINRA, peer-reviewed academic studies of retail trader performance in several countries, and the freely available Berkshire Hathaway shareholder letters. Nothing in this book asks the reader to take a number on faith.

Why a second edition

The first edition of this book was a warning. It described what happens to ordinary people who get pulled into day trading. The argument has not changed. What has changed is the depth of the explanation. The first edition told readers that day trading is risky. The second edition explains, in plain language, why the math, the markets, the brokers, the apps, and the human mind all push the same way.

If a reader finished the first edition convinced and walked away, the first edition did its job. If a reader finished the first edition curious about why the warning works, this second edition is meant for them.

Who this book is for

This book is for the person thinking about starting. It is for the person already trading and quietly losing. It is for the spouse, parent, or friend who can see a pattern forming in someone they care about and is looking for words to use. It is also for readers who simply want to understand how modern markets actually work, what the data say about retail outcomes, and what a calmer alternative looks like.

It is not for professional traders working at institutions, who already know most of what is in here. It is not for sophisticated investors managing eight-figure portfolios with a team of advisors. The audience is ordinary people with ordinary savings, in a world where a phone can place a leveraged trade in three taps.

What success actually looks like

It is worth saying out loud what financial success usually looks like for ordinary people, because the version sold online is misleading. Most people who end up financially comfortable in their fifties or sixties do not get there through trading. They get there through a steady job, a steady savings rate, a low-cost diversified portfolio, a paid-off home, and the absence of catastrophic events. Their portfolios were never thrilling. Their stories do not make good content. They are, in aggregate, the population that lives the longest, sleeps the best, and worries the least about money in retirement.

The version of success that fills social media — the screenshot of a six-figure trading day, the new car, the lifestyle behind a curated camera — is real for a tiny minority and unrealistic for almost everyone else. The boring version is achievable for the majority of people willing to follow a simple plan over decades. The exciting version is achievable for very few, and most of the people pursuing it end up with neither version. They end up with a depleted account, a stressful decade, and the realization that the boring path was always available.

About sources and citations

This book uses citations sparingly. Where a number or claim is empirical, the source is footnoted at the end of the chapter where the claim appears. Where the source is a regulatory page, the URL is included. Where the source is an academic paper, the DOI or stable link is provided. The point of the citations is not to make the book look academic. It is to let you check anything you want to verify. Most of what is in here can be cross-checked in a few minutes with a search engine and a willingness to read the underlying source.

The Berkshire Hathaway shareholder letters are referenced in several places. They are free, they are online, and they cumulatively contain more useful investing wisdom than almost any paid course. A reader who finishes this book and reads ten years of those letters has done something significant for their own financial education that did not cost a dollar.

Why this book is short on certainties

If you are looking for a book that promises a system, this is the wrong one. The honest writer on day trading does not promise a system because no system reliably delivers what the marketing claims. What an honest book can offer is the structure of the problem: what kinds of activities produce reliable financial outcomes, what kinds usually do not, and why the difference is what it is.

Reading this book will not make you a profitable day trader. Nothing will, for most readers. What it can do is help you make a clearer decision about whether to participate at all, at what size, with what protections, and with what alternative paths in place. That is a more modest promise than the marketing version, and it is the only one this book is willing to keep.

How to use the rest of this book

Each chapter is short enough to finish in one sitting. The chapters build on each other, but each one also stands on its own. A reader short on time can pick the chapters that match the question they actually have. Worried about a friend who seems to be drifting into compulsive trading? Skip ahead to the chapters on addiction and personal relationships. Trying to decide whether to start? Read the methods, markets, and costs chapters first. Already trading and uncertain whether to continue? Track every trade for thirty days, compute the realized cost after fees, and then read the chapter on hidden fees with that number in front of you.

The book is also designed to be re-read. Most people who read it once and act will not get every benefit. The ideas tend to land harder the second time, when the reader has tried something and seen the results. If a chapter does not connect on first read, set it aside. Come back when life has supplied an example.

A note on tone

This book takes a firm position. Day trading, on the data, is bad for the people who try it. The author has spent enough time looking at the evidence and the human costs to feel comfortable saying so plainly. Some readers will find that tone uncomfortable. They are welcome to disagree. The disagreement does not change the data, but it is honest, and the book is written in the spirit of leaving room for it.

What the book is not willing to do is soften the message into something that pretends both sides are equal. They are not. The data is one-sided. Hedging the conclusion to seem balanced would be dishonest, and dishonesty in service of comfort is exactly the failure mode this book is trying to help readers avoid. The path to a calmer financial life often starts with hearing something uncomfortable clearly, rather than hearing it gently and ignoring it.

Chapter 2

Day Trading Methods

Day trading is not one thing. It is a family of styles, each with its own rhythm, time frame, and risk profile. Knowing the differences helps in two ways. First, it makes the marketing easier to see through. Most courses and gurus are selling one specific style and presenting it as the whole craft. Second, it helps you spot which style, if any, suits the time and money you actually have.

Below are the main approaches you will run into. Each gets a short, honest description: what it is, how it works, and where it tends to go wrong.

Scalping

Scalping means making many small trades, often dozens or even hundreds in a session, holding each one for seconds or minutes. The goal is to capture tiny price moves and let them add up. The math sounds appealing — small wins, but lots of them. The reality is harder. Every round trip pays the spread between the bid and the ask, plus any slippage and any commissions. On thin moves, those costs eat the edge before it shows up. Scalpers compete directly with professional market makers and high-speed firms whose entire business is being faster and cheaper than everyone else. Most retail scalpers are paying fees to compete in a race they cannot win.

Range trading

Range traders look for a price level a stock or currency keeps bouncing off (the floor, called support) and another it keeps backing away from (the ceiling, called resistance). They buy near the floor and sell near the ceiling. When the range holds, the trade works. When the price breaks out of the range — which it eventually does — the same trader can lose more on one breakout than they made over weeks of clean bounces. Range trading rewards calm markets and punishes news days.

News trading

News traders try to ride the price reaction to a headline: an earnings report, a Federal Reserve announcement, a major economic release, a takeover rumor. The first move usually happens in seconds. Professional desks have machine-readable news feeds that parse the release and place orders before a human can read the first sentence. Retail traders typing quickly arrive after the first move and often end up trading the second move, which is whatever the professionals decide to do next. Trading the news is one of the easier ways to learn how slow your phone really is.

Momentum trading

Momentum traders follow stocks that are already moving sharply. The thinking is that strong moves often continue for a while as more buyers (or sellers) pile in. There is some truth to it over weeks and months. Inside a single day, the signal is much weaker, and momentum trades on small-cap names are a favorite playground for promoters who pump a stock, sell into the buying, and leave the late arrivals holding the loss.

Position and swing trading

Position trading and swing trading hold trades for days, weeks, or sometimes months. Strictly speaking, neither one is really day trading, but most people who call themselves day traders dabble in both. The longer holding period reduces the number of trades, which reduces transaction costs and stress, but it adds overnight risk: news can break while you sleep, and the market can open at a price your stop never gets a chance to catch.

High-frequency and algorithmic trading

High-frequency trading uses computer programs to place thousands of trades per second, often holding positions for milliseconds. Algorithmic trading is the broader category — any rules-based, computer-executed trading. Both are real and both are dominated by professional firms with co-located servers, custom hardware, and teams of engineers. When a retail product advertises "algorithmic trading" or "AI trading" for a monthly fee, it is almost never the same activity. It is a script with a marketing budget.

Arbitrage

Arbitrage tries to capture small price differences for the same asset across different markets — for example, a stock priced slightly higher on one exchange than another, or a cryptocurrency listed on two venues at different prices. Real arbitrage is fast and competitive. By the time a retail trader sees a difference, professional firms with faster connections have usually closed it. The cases that look big enough for a person to chase by hand are usually too thin or too risky once fees and transfer times are counted.

Options trading

Options give the buyer the right (not the duty) to buy or sell an asset at a set price by a set date. They are powerful tools and dangerous in inexperienced hands. Buying short-dated options near expiration looks cheap because the price tags are small. The expected value, after the spread and after time decay, is typically negative for the buyer. The few who win big show up loudly on social media. The many who lose every cent of premium do not post.

What unites every style

Despite the variety, every day-trading style shares the same underlying problem. Each trade pays costs — the spread, possible slippage, sometimes commissions, often financing if leverage is involved. To make money, the trader's edge has to beat all those costs and still leave a profit. The time horizon is so short that the underlying business or asset has no time to grow into the position; the price simply has to move the right way before the close.

That is the hidden coin flip behind every chart and every system. The next chapter looks at the markets where these games are played and what is special about each one.

Why every method shares the same problem

The styles in this chapter look different on the screen. They are not as different underneath. Every one of them depends on guessing where a price will move in the next minute, hour, or day. Every one pays the spread between the bid and the ask each time the trader enters and exits. Every one competes against professional firms whose entire business is being faster, cheaper, and better-informed.

The marketing of each style emphasizes its strength. Scalping promises many small wins. Momentum promises the thrill of a strong move. News trading promises a fast catalyst.

What the marketing rarely says is that all of these styles share the same underlying weakness. The trader has to be right often enough, by enough, to overcome costs that arrive on every single round trip. Most retail traders do not clear that bar over time.

A simple way to test any method

Before risking real money, calculate the round-trip cost of one trade in the chosen method. Add the bid-ask spread, the average slippage, any commission, and any overnight financing if the trade is held past the close. Multiply by the expected number of trades per month. Compare that monthly cost to a realistic estimate of what the method is supposed to earn. The answer is usually sobering.

If the cost of trading the method comes close to the expected return, the method has no real edge. It is a coin flip with extra steps. If the cost exceeds the expected return, the method is a slow, certain way to lose money. This kind of arithmetic is not exciting, but it tells you more than any chart pattern.

The marketing trap

Every retail trading style has at least one well-known instructor selling a course on it. The course features screenshots of profitable trades, testimonials from happy students, and a price tag that often climbs into thousands of dollars. The reasoning behind buying a course is straightforward — you want to learn — but the economics of the course business should give pause.

An instructor who can sign up a thousand subscribers at fifty dollars a month earns six hundred thousand dollars a year from the subscription alone, win or lose, regardless of whether their actual trading account makes money. That economic reality shapes the marketing. The instructor optimizes for sign-ups, not for student outcomes. Some instructors are honest about this. Many are not. A reader trying to choose a teacher should look for verified, audited track records, transparent pricing, and a willingness to recommend free resources first.

What changes between practice and live trading

Many trading platforms offer paper-trading accounts that simulate placing trades without using real money. They are useful for learning the mechanics of an interface and for testing whether a strategy works in principle. They are misleading in one important way: paper trading does not feel like real trading.

When the money is not real, the trader sizes positions a little larger, holds losers a little longer, and takes profits a little later, because none of the decisions matter emotionally. When the same trader switches to live trading with real money, the decisions feel completely different. The same setup that produced calm clicks in the simulator produces sweat, hesitation, and overrides in the live account. Many traders who looked profitable on paper become unprofitable in real trading not because the strategy stopped working but because they cannot execute it the same way under emotional pressure.

If you intend to trade with real money, the honest path is to start with a small live account rather than a paper account. The amount can be tiny — a few hundred dollars — but the dollars must be real. The cost of the lesson is small, and the lesson itself is unavoidable. Better to learn it on a small account than to discover it after scaling up from a backtest that never accounted for nervous-system effects.

Time of day matters

Most retail trading days have predictable rhythm. The first thirty minutes after the open are the most volatile and the highest-volume. Spreads are wider then because the market is still digesting overnight news and quotes are repricing. Around the middle of the session, volume typically thins, and price movements become more random. The last thirty minutes are active again, with closing flows from large funds and last-minute hedging.

Many retail traders, attracted by the volatility of the open, take their largest positions in exactly the moments when costs are highest and the chance of getting a clean fill is lowest. The result is a pattern of small wins on calmer days and larger losses on the volatile ones, because the volatile days are the ones the trader cannot help participating in. Choosing not to trade the open is one of the cheapest improvements a retail trader can make to their own results.

How to evaluate any new method honestly

Every few months, a new trading method appears in the retail conversation. Some are old methods rebranded. Some use new vocabulary borrowed from machine learning, options theory, or whatever the current technology theme provides. The marketing makes each one sound like the answer that previous methods were missing.

A small set of questions cuts through most of the marketing. Does this method have a documented edge after realistic transaction costs? Has it been tested on data the rule was not developed against? Are the people teaching it deploying it with their own substantial capital, and does their wealth visibly come from trading rather than from teaching? Does the method's logic hold up to a few minutes of skeptical reading, or does it depend on hand-waving about why "the markets have changed"? Most new methods fail several of these questions. The few that survive are usually old methods, well known to professionals, with too small an edge to support the level of marketing being applied to them.

What it costs to learn each method properly

Each method described in this chapter has a learning curve measured in months and years, not days. Scalping requires real-time pattern recognition that takes hundreds of hours of screen time to develop, and the patterns that work in one volatility regime stop working in another. Momentum trading requires the trader to learn the difference between a real breakout and a false one, which usually means living through several false ones with real money. Options trading requires understanding non-linear payoffs and time decay, which most retail traders never fully internalize.

The honest cost of learning is not the price of a course. It is the months or years of mediocre results while the trader builds the actual judgment. Most people who start trading do not survive that period. They either run out of money, run out of patience, or convince themselves that they have learned what they have not. The few who do survive often discover that the realized edge, once they have it, is too small to justify the time it took to build. They could have spent the same hours on more reliable financial activities and ended up further ahead.

Why even good methods rarely survive at retail

Suppose, for the sake of argument, that one of the methods in this chapter does have a small real edge for a careful practitioner. The edge has to survive a long series of difficulties before it produces money in a retail account. It has to survive realistic transaction costs. It has to survive the trader's emotional reaction to losing trades. It has to survive periods of underperformance long enough to test anyone's patience. It has to survive the trader switching strategies after a few bad weeks, which most retail traders eventually do.

Even small edges, in disciplined hands, can produce decent results. The disciplined hands are the rare part. Most retail traders, including ones who genuinely understand the methods they are using, do not maintain the discipline long enough to benefit from whatever edge their method might offer. The method is not the binding constraint. The trader is.

A short reading list for each method

Each style described in this chapter has a small body of serious literature behind it, and a much larger body of marketing material in front of it. A reader genuinely curious about a method should read the serious version first. For market microstructure and the realities of execution, academic papers are freely available through search engines that index research repositories. For options, several textbook-style introductions exist that explain the math honestly without trying to sell anything. For futures, the exchanges themselves publish educational materials. The serious literature is unglamorous, often dense, and accurate. The marketing literature is the opposite on all three. The reader who starts with the serious version has a much better foundation for evaluating any specific course or system later.

Chapter 3

Day Trading Markets

A trader can place a market order on dozens of different markets. Each one has its own rules, its own players, its own opening hours, and its own way of taking money from people who do not understand the structure. This chapter walks through the main ones in plain language.

Stocks

Stock markets are where shares of public companies trade. In the United States, the main exchanges are the New York Stock Exchange and Nasdaq. Other countries have their own. For a day trader, only a small slice of the listed universe matters. Out of thousands of listed names, a few hundred have enough daily volume and tight enough spreads to enter and exit quickly without giving up too much on costs. Everyone else is competing for the same handful of names every day.

U.S. retail stock orders mostly go through commission-free brokers. "Free" does not mean free; the broker is paid by wholesale market makers for the right to fill your order. The arrangement is legal and disclosed in fine print, but it means your trades are routed through a system that earns more when you trade more.

Foreign exchange (forex)

The foreign exchange market is the largest financial market in the world by volume. Most of that volume is between banks and big institutions. The retail forex market is a separate world that runs alongside it, often with very different mechanics. In the U.S., regulators cap retail leverage at fifty to one for major currency pairs and twenty to one for minor pairs. Outside the U.S., it is common to see one hundred to one or higher. At those levels, a small move against you wipes out the whole account.

Many retail forex brokers also act as the trader's counterparty. When you buy, they sell. When you lose, they often gain. There are honest exceptions, but the basic incentive structure is worth knowing before you put money in.

Futures

Futures are contracts to buy or sell an asset at a set price on a future date. Index futures (like the E-mini S&P 500), commodity futures (oil, gold, corn), and currency futures all attract day traders. Futures trade on regulated exchanges with a single, transparent order book — the same one institutions use, which is fairer than the retail forex setup. The catch is leverage. A single E-mini S&P contract represents hundreds of thousands of dollars of exposure, and many brokers let small traders hold it on a few hundred dollars of margin. A normal day in the index can produce a swing larger than the trader's whole account.

Options

Options trade on stocks, indexes, exchange-traded funds, and futures. They have non-linear payoffs, which means the price does not move the same amount as the underlying asset. They lose value as expiration approaches if the underlying does not cooperate. They gain or lose value when the market's expected volatility shifts, even if nothing else changes. New traders often understand the first feature, ignore the second, and discover the third by losing money.

Cryptocurrencies

Crypto markets trade twenty-four hours a day, seven days a week, across hundreds of venues. There is no single tape, no consolidated quote, no automatic protections. Liquidity is concentrated in the largest coins. Smaller tokens often have wide spreads, thin order books, and structural risks that the price chart does not show. There is also no FDIC for crypto exchanges. When one fails — and the list of failures is long — customer balances become unsecured claims in a bankruptcy that may take years to resolve.

Picking your battlefield

It is tempting to think that one market is safer than the others. The truth is that each one has its own version of the same problem: costs you do not see clearly, leverage that lets a small mistake become a big one, and professional players who have an edge you do not. A different market does not change the basic math. It only changes which way you are most likely to be hurt.

The next chapter takes a step back and looks at the much larger choice behind all of this — the difference between trading and investing, and why so many people who think they are doing one are really doing the other.

What "liquidity" really means

Liquidity is one of those market words that sounds technical but means something simple. A liquid asset is one you can buy or sell quickly without moving the price much. A liquid stock has many buyers and sellers showing up every minute, ready to trade. An illiquid stock might go for hours with very few orders, which means a single order can shift the price by a noticeable amount.

Liquidity matters because it determines what you actually pay to enter and exit. In a liquid market, the gap between the highest price a buyer is willing to pay and the lowest a seller is willing to take is small. In an illiquid market, the gap is wide. A trader who buys an illiquid stock at the asking price and tries to sell five minutes later often discovers that the only available buyer is offering significantly less. The difference is not a fee, exactly. It is just the cost of being in a thin market.

Trading hours and overnight risk

Each market has its own hours. U.S. stocks trade primarily between 9:30 and 4:00 Eastern. Futures trade nearly around the clock with a short pause. Forex runs from Sunday evening to Friday afternoon. Crypto never stops. Hours matter for two reasons. First, liquidity is concentrated during the busiest part of the session, and trading at quieter times means wider spreads and more slippage. Second, holding a position overnight means accepting the risk that something will happen while you cannot react — an earnings release, a war headline, a regulatory ruling. The next morning's open can sit far from the previous night's close, with no chance for a stop-loss to catch the move at the level you set.

The pattern day trader rule, plainly

In the United States, FINRA designates an account a "pattern day trader" once it makes four or more day trades in any five-business-day period, where those day trades are more than six percent of the account's total trading. Once an account is flagged, it must hold at least twenty-five thousand dollars in equity and is restricted to trading at no more than four times its maintenance margin excess intraday.

The rule sounds annoying. Many trading instructors sell techniques to work around it. The rule exists because, after years of observing what happens to small accounts that day trade actively, regulators decided that small undercapitalized day trading is the most reliably destructive form of retail activity. The minimum equity requirement is not a barrier to opportunity. It is a quiet warning that this activity does not work well for small balances.

Choosing what not to trade

A common mistake among new traders is to trade everything available. The brokerage app shows a menu of stocks, options, futures, crypto, and forex, and the trader rotates through them in search of "the one that works." Each rotation pays new costs, demands fresh learning, and accumulates new losses.

A better approach, if you trade at all, is to pick one market, learn its specific rules, and stay in it. The losses you take in any single market come from a handful of recognizable patterns. The losses you take across many markets come from many patterns at once, and the lessons do not transfer cleanly between them. Choosing what not to trade is one of the cheaper decisions a trader can make. It costs nothing and removes a meaningful share of the worst outcomes.

Why some markets favor patient capital

Some markets are structurally easier for long-term investors and structurally harder for short-term traders. Broad-market index funds are the clearest example. They benefit from the long-run productivity of the underlying companies, automatic dividend reinvestment, and the reduced impact of any single company's bad year. The patient holder is paid by the system. The day trader, in the same instrument, has to overcome costs that the patient holder does not pay, against participants who are usually better-equipped.

This is not an argument that all markets favor patient capital. Some, like the spot foreign-exchange market, are essentially zero-sum at the level retail can access. The point is that the choice of market is not neutral. A reader who tilts their financial life toward markets that reward patience and away from markets that punish it is making one of the most important decisions in their financial planning, even if they never think of it that way.

Margin requirements and what they mean

When a broker says a position requires "twenty-five percent margin," they mean that the trader must hold equity equal to twenty-five percent of the position's value. The other seventy-five percent is effectively borrowed from the broker. As the position fluctuates, the equity requirement does too, and if the trader's equity falls below the maintenance margin level, the broker can sell the position to bring the account back into compliance.

These rules exist for a reason. Without them, brokers would extend credit endlessly, and customers would lose more money than they could repay. The rules also mean that a trader on margin is operating in a system where the broker has the final word on whether positions stay open. A market move that triggers a maintenance call at the worst possible moment is not a bug. It is exactly how the system is supposed to work, and the trader is the one who agreed to play by those rules when they opened the margin account.

Why "choose your market" is a financial decision

When a reader chooses which market to participate in, they are making a financial planning decision more consequential than most realize. Some markets — diversified equity index funds, broad bond funds — are structurally hospitable to long-term investors. They tend to grow over decades, the costs of holding are low, the regulatory framework is mature, and the participants on the other side of trades are mostly other patient investors with similar goals.

Other markets — high-leverage retail forex, low-volume small-cap stocks, illiquid token markets — are structurally hostile to retail. The costs are high, the leverage is extreme, the regulation is weaker, and the participants on the other side often have informational and structural advantages. A reader who tilts their financial life toward the first kind of market and away from the second has changed the entire risk profile of their financial life, often without realizing it. This single decision matters more than any specific stock pick.

Why simulators feel different from real markets

Most brokerages offer demo or paper-trading accounts. They are useful for learning the buttons. They are misleading in one important way: the trader does not feel the actual costs. A paper-trading platform will fill an order at the displayed quote even when, in real markets, the order would have moved the price slightly. It will not show the trader the slippage that real orders incur. It will not include the small but real delays between deciding to trade and the trade actually being executed. It will simulate fills for orders that, in real markets, would have been partially filled or not filled at all.

The result is that strategies that look profitable in simulation often turn out to be break-even or losing in real markets, because the simulator was generous about the things real markets are stingy about. The honest test of any new strategy is to deploy it with real money in very small size for several months, before scaling up. The cost of the test is small. The information it produces is real, in a way that simulator data is not.

Why one market is enough

Beginning traders often diversify across several markets at once, telling themselves that a multi-market approach reduces risk. The reasoning is wrong. Each new market adds learning costs, new platforms, new vocabulary, new failure modes, and new ways to lose money. The trader's attention is finite. Spreading it across multiple markets means each market gets less attention, not more, and the inevitable mistakes happen more often as a result.

The honest discipline is to pick one market that fits the trader's available time and risk tolerance and stay there until they understand it deeply. Even then, the deep understanding is unlikely to produce profits, given the structural disadvantages described elsewhere in this book. But understanding one market well at least lets the trader fail efficiently. Spreading thin across several markets ensures inefficient failure on multiple fronts at once.

Why most retail traders concentrate in the worst markets

There is an unfortunate selection effect in retail trading. The markets that are hardest on retail — high-leverage retail forex, low-volume small-cap stocks, freshly launched crypto tokens, zero-day options — are also the markets where the marketing is loudest, the apparent payoffs are largest, and the path to participation is easiest. The result is that the markets that should attract retail least attract them most. The patient, structurally favorable markets — broad index funds, large-cap stocks held long-term, investment-grade bonds — receive less retail attention because they are boring. The boring markets are the ones that produce the better outcomes. The selection effect runs in exactly the wrong direction for retail welfare.

Chapter 4

Day trading Versus Investment

Trading and investing get used as if they mean the same thing. They do not. The difference between them is the most important single idea in this book, and it is worth spending a chapter to make plain.

What investing actually is

An investment is a piece of a real, productive business. When you own shares of a company through a broad fund, you own a tiny fraction of the offices, the workers, the brand, and the future earnings. Over years and decades, those earnings grow. The owners of the businesses, in aggregate, get paid by that growth — through dividends, through reinvested profits, through rising share prices that reflect the growing value of what they own.

An investor does not need the price to move tomorrow. The investor's reward shows up over years, not minutes. The investor's job is to pick assets sensibly, hold them through cycles, and stay out of their own way.

What day trading actually is

A day trade is not a piece of a business. It is a short bet that the price will move the right way before the close. The trader's reward depends on the price move alone, not on anything the underlying business produces. The position is closed before the company has time to earn anything for the trader.

That makes day trading a different activity from investing, even when the asset on the screen is the same stock. Same screen, same ticker, very different game.

A line that has held up for seventy-five years

Benjamin Graham, the writer who taught Warren Buffett, drew this line carefully in his book *The Intelligent Investor*. In our own words: a real investment is one you make after thinking carefully about what you are buying, with reasonable confidence that your money is protected and that you will earn an acceptable return over time. If those things are not true, you are speculating. Speculation is not always wrong, but it should be sized small, kept separate, and never confused with investing.

Graham's point was practical. Many people who think they are investing are actually speculating, because they have done little analysis and have no real protection against being wrong. Many people who think they are too cautious to invest are actually well suited to it, because the patient, ordinary version of investing is much calmer than the cable-news version.

The Buffett version

Warren Buffett built a long career on a simple version of the same idea. Buy pieces of good businesses you understand. Pay a price that leaves room for being wrong. Hold for a long time. Let the businesses do the work.

Buffett also gives one practical piece of advice for almost everyone who is not a professional investor: buy a low-cost index fund that owns the whole market, add to it regularly, and leave it alone. That is not a fashion or a theory. It is what he has put in writing in the public Berkshire Hathaway shareholder letters, and it is what he has said his own estate is instructed to do with cash left for his family. The advice is free, repeated for decades, and ignored by most retail traders the moment they download a trading app.

Why patience wins on the math

Compounding is the quiet engine behind real investing. A reasonable rate of return, applied to your money year after year, doubles it roughly every nine to ten years. Two doublings turn a starting amount into four times itself. Three doublings turn it into eight. Across a working life, the difference between earning an honest middle-of-the-road return for thirty years and trying to chase higher returns through trading can be enormous — often in favor of the boring path.

There is also an asymmetry that punishes traders. Losses hurt more than gains help. A fifty percent loss requires a one hundred percent gain just to get back to even. A seventy-five percent loss needs a three hundred percent gain. Survival is not just nice to have. It is the precondition for compounding to work at all.

Where speculation fits

Speculation is not forbidden. Graham himself said it has a place. The honest version of it has three rules: use only money you can afford to lose, keep the speculative account walled off from your real savings, and never let a bad week tempt you to top it up from somewhere it should not come from. Following those three rules turns speculation into a hobby. Breaking them turns it into the family-sized disaster the rest of this book describes.

The choice this book is really about

Most of the rest of this book is a careful look at what happens when speculation is mistaken for investment. The remaining chapters cover the markets, the tools, the costs, and the human toll. The last chapter comes back to investing in the Graham-and-Buffett sense and shows what a calmer, simpler path looks like in practice.

If you take only one idea from this chapter, take this: the short-term price chart is not the source of long-term wealth. The productive growth of real businesses, owned patiently, is. The chart is the noise. The growth is the signal. Almost every mistake in this book starts with confusing the two.

What compounding actually does

Compounding is the simple idea that money earns money, and the money earned then earns more money. The interesting part is what compounding does over long periods of time. A dollar earning eight percent a year doubles in about nine years. Two doublings turn a dollar into four. Three doublings turn it into eight. Four doublings turn it into sixteen. Across a working life of thirty or forty years, the same dollar contributed steadily can grow into something the contributor never quite expected when they started.

The numbers feel small in any single year. That is what makes compounding hard to use. A patient investor watches the account grow by a little, sometimes by nothing, sometimes by less than nothing in a bad year, and has to keep contributing anyway. The reward shows up at the far end. The trader who chases excitement gives up that quiet engine entirely. Whatever they earn day by day, they earn alone, without the silent help of time.

Buffett's actual recommendation

Warren Buffett, who is rich enough to invest however he wants, has been remarkably consistent about what he recommends for everyone else. In his Berkshire Hathaway shareholder letters, he writes that most non-professional investors are best served by putting their money into a low-cost broad-market index fund — one that owns small pieces of hundreds or thousands of public companies — and leaving it there for decades. He says he has given his own family the same instruction in writing for the cash they will inherit.

His reasoning is plain. The average professional fund manager underperforms a simple index fund after costs. The typical retail investor does worse than the funds, because they buy when they feel optimistic and sell when they feel scared. The index fund avoids both layers of cost. It does not promise to make anyone rich quickly. It promises something less exciting and more reliable: a share of whatever the broad economy produces over time, captured cheaply, without the investor having to be smart about market timing.

Graham's two kinds of investor

Benjamin Graham wrote that there are two kinds of investors. The first he called the defensive investor — someone who wants a reasonable return without spending a lot of time and effort, and without making big mistakes. The second he called the enterprising investor — someone willing to do the work of analyzing individual businesses, in the hope of doing a little better than average.

Most readers, if they are honest about how much time they actually have, are the first kind. That is fine. Graham's advice for the defensive investor was to own a balanced portfolio of stocks and bonds, contribute to it regularly, rebalance once in a while, and resist the urge to chase fashionable ideas. The modern version of that advice is a low-cost index fund or a target-date fund. It is not flashy. It is the most reliable thing on the menu.

The Mr. Market story, retold

Graham used a simple story to explain what the stock market actually is. Imagine you own a small share of a private business, alongside a partner. Every day, this partner shows up at your door and names a price at which he will either buy your share or sell you more. Some days he is excited and quotes a high price. Some days he is gloomy and quotes a low one. The price has nothing to do with the business itself. It is just his mood for the day.

If you are a real owner of the business, you do not let his mood decide what your share is worth. You have your own view, based on what the business is actually doing. You only deal with him when his price is plainly good for you — buying more when his quote is unusually low, perhaps selling some when his quote is unusually high. The rest of the time, his daily quotes are background noise.

That is what the stock market is. The day-by-day price is one nervous partner shouting numbers. The investor's job is not to follow his moods. It is to know what the underlying assets are actually worth and to act only when his prices are useful. Day trading is the opposite — it is taking the partner's mood as the only thing that matters and trying to guess what mood he will be in five minutes from now.

Margin of safety, in plain English

Another idea Graham emphasized is what he called margin of safety. The phrase sounds technical. The meaning is simple: when you buy something, pay a price that gives you room to be wrong. If you estimate that a business is worth ten dollars a share and the market is asking seven, you have three dollars of cushion. If your estimate turns out to be too optimistic — and estimates often are — the cushion absorbs some of the error. If you estimate the same value and pay nine dollars and fifty cents, there is almost no cushion at all. Any mistake in your estimate becomes a real loss.

Margin of safety is not a magic phrase. It is a habit. The investor who insists on a wide cushion buys less often, because most assets do not trade at a meaningful discount most of the time. The patience that this requires is exactly the patience day trading does not allow. Day traders cannot wait years for a good price. They have to act today, on whatever the market is offering, with no protection if their guess is wrong.

Why this distinction is the most important one in the book

If you take only one idea from these pages, take this. The short-term price chart is not the source of long-term wealth. Real wealth, for the kind of person reading a book like this one, is built by owning small pieces of productive businesses for a long time, contributing regularly, and refusing to be talked into clever-sounding alternatives. Almost every mistake described in the chapters that follow starts with confusing speculation for investment. The two activities use the same words, the same screens, sometimes even the same brokerage account. They are not the same thing.

The 'circle of competence' idea

Buffett often describes what he calls the circle of competence. The phrase sounds technical and means something simple: invest in things you can actually understand. The size of your circle matters less than knowing where its edges are. Many investors with narrow but real understanding have done well over time. Many investors with broad but shallow understanding have done poorly. Knowing what you do not know is more useful than pretending to know more than you do.

For most readers, the honest circle of competence is small. They understand a little about the company they work for, perhaps the industry they work in, perhaps a few household-name businesses they have watched for years. They do not understand emerging markets, biotech research pipelines, derivatives strategies, or whatever the trending sector happens to be this quarter. The discipline of staying inside the circle, and using a low-cost index fund for everything outside it, is one of the most reliable habits in patient investing. The temptation to wander outside the circle, because something looks exciting, is one of the most reliable sources of error.

Time horizon as a competitive advantage

Long time horizon is one of the few real competitive advantages an ordinary investor has over a professional. Most professional fund managers are evaluated quarterly. They cannot afford a poor quarter, even if their long-term thesis is intact, because clients leave when results lag. The pressure forces them into shorter-term thinking than they would otherwise prefer.

An individual investor with a thirty-year horizon does not have those constraints. They can hold through a bad year, a bad three years, even a bad decade, if the underlying thesis is sound. This advantage is largely wasted by retail traders who voluntarily compress their horizon to minutes and hours. The horizon was the asset. They gave it away to chase the volatility a professional with a different incentive structure has to chase. The patient holder, with no quarterly review and no client redemptions, simply waits — and wait, in markets, is paid.

What the index actually owns

Some readers feel uneasy buying "the market" through an index fund because they cannot picture what they actually own. A clarification helps. A total U.S. stock market index fund holds small pieces of roughly the largest three thousand publicly traded U.S. companies, weighted by their size. When you put a hundred dollars into it, you become a tiny fractional owner of Apple, Microsoft, JPMorgan Chase, Procter & Gamble, ExxonMobil, your local utility, the food company that made your breakfast, and so on, down to companies you have never heard of.

Across decades, those companies, in aggregate, generate earnings, pay dividends, reinvest in their businesses, and grow. The index fund collects all of that on your behalf, automatically, with almost no effort on your part. Owning the index is owning a small piece of the productive economy. It is the simplest, cheapest version of what real investing actually is.

Why the patient path actually works

It is worth pausing to ask why the patient path produces such consistent results across decades and across investors with different temperaments. The answer is not that patient investors are smarter. Many of them know less about markets than the average day trader. The answer is structural.

Patient investors capture the underlying productivity of real businesses. They pay almost no transaction costs. They generate almost no taxable events. They do not have to predict short-term movements. They benefit from compounding for the longest possible time horizon. They make few enough decisions that emotion has fewer chances to interfere. They have lower stress, which means better health, which means longer time in the market. Each of these structural features is small in any given year. Compounded across forty years, they produce outcomes that no level of trading skill can reliably match in the same household.

What if the market falls right after I start

A common worry from new investors is that they will start contributing right before a major market decline and watch their savings evaporate. The worry is reasonable, and the answer is reassuring. A new investor making automatic monthly contributions is buying through the decline, which means they are accumulating shares at lower prices. When the market eventually recovers — and historically it always has, eventually — those low-priced shares produce most of the gains.

The investor who started right before the 2008 financial crisis, kept contributing, and held through, ended up with an excellent ten-year result, because their later contributions bought heavily discounted shares that compounded as the market healed. The investor who started in 2008 and panicked out at the bottom locked in losses and missed the recovery. The difference between the two outcomes was not the timing. It was the behavior. Behavior, not timing, is what most patient investors actually have to manage.

What "long-term" actually means in numbers

Long-term, in investing, is a phrase that gets used loosely. The honest version has a specific meaning. Over any one-year period, broad-market stock returns can be anywhere from substantially negative to substantially positive. Over any five-year period, the range narrows but is still wide. Over any twenty-year period in modern market history, broad diversified equity portfolios have produced positive returns, after inflation, in nearly every case. Over thirty-year periods, the range narrows further and the average is meaningful.

The implication is that the long-term investor's edge is real, but it requires actually holding for the long term. An investor who holds for one year is not getting the benefit. An investor who panics out during the first major decline is not getting it. The benefit shows up at the far end of patient discipline, applied through several market cycles. The day trader cannot capture any of this, because they sell every position before the long-term effects begin to operate. Time is the variable that separates the two activities. It is also the variable most retail traders do not value highly enough.

What good investing looks like in a single year

On a year-by-year basis, good investing is often boring. The investor contributes the planned amount each month. They do not check the account daily. They do not react to news. They rebalance once a year if the allocation has drifted. They watch the broad market do whatever it does. Some years the account grows nicely. Some years it falls. The investor adjusts none of their contributions in response. They keep doing the same thing month after month.

This is not glamorous. It is also what builds wealth at scale across decades. The investor who, looking back at thirty years, did this consistently is in a much better position than the investor who tried to do something cleverer in any individual year. The boring approach has a hidden virtue: it is sustainable. The clever approaches usually are not.

What history says about long horizons

Looking at long-run market data is sobering for short-term traders and reassuring for long-term investors. Across periods of twenty years or more in modern market history, broad diversified equity portfolios have produced positive real returns in essentially all rolling periods, in essentially all developed markets, even when the period included a major crash, a recession, or a war. The long horizon is what makes the underlying productivity show through the noise.

This does not guarantee that the next twenty years will look like the last hundred. Past results are not a promise. But the consistency of the long-horizon record across very different historical periods is striking. The same strategy that worked through the Great Depression also worked through the post-war expansion, the inflation of the 1970s, the financial crisis of 2008, and the pandemic of 2020. None of those periods was easy in the moment. The strategy survived them all because it was anchored to something real — the underlying productive output of real businesses — rather than to any specific theory about what was about to happen.

How the patient path looks year by year

Year by year, patient investing is unremarkable. In good years, the portfolio rises, sometimes substantially. In bad years, it falls, sometimes substantially. The investor adjusts almost nothing. They do not feel particularly clever after good years and they do not feel particularly stupid after bad ones. They simply continue the pattern of contributing, holding, and ignoring most of what they read in financial media.

Across many such years, the boring pattern produces a result that no individual year would have predicted. The compounding shows up at the far end. The investor looking back from retirement at thirty years of patient discipline often does not remember any specific year as decisive. The result was the cumulative effect of consistent behavior, not any particular trade or insight. This is the nature of the patient path. It does not produce moments. It produces outcomes.

Chapter 5

Factors Influencing the Market and Prices

Every chart you look at is the result of millions of decisions, made for thousands of reasons, by people and machines you cannot see. To trade the chart is to bet that you understand those decisions better than the people making them. This chapter walks through the main forces that move prices, in plain language, so you can see why short-term forecasting is so difficult.

Interest rates and central banks

Interest rates set by central banks are the gravitational pull of financial markets. When rates rise, the present value of future cash flows falls, and most asset prices come down with it. When rates fall, the same math runs in reverse. A central bank meeting can reset the value of stocks, bonds, currencies, and real estate in minutes. Most of the time, traders are not just reacting to the actual decision but to small changes in what the next decision is expected to be. That is why a single sentence in a Federal Reserve statement can move trillions of dollars.

Inflation and growth

Inflation reports tell the market what the central bank is likely to do next. A higher-than-expected number raises rate fears and pushes stock prices down. A softer number does the opposite. Growth numbers — jobs, retail sales, factory output — set the level of corporate earnings the market is willing to pay for. The same data point can produce opposite reactions depending on what the market was already expecting. "Good news is bad news" and "bad news is good news" are not jokes; they describe how a market that watches the central bank reacts to surprises.

Earnings and company news

Individual stocks rise and fall on their own news: quarterly earnings, guidance about future quarters, new contracts, lawsuits, regulatory rulings, management changes. A single earnings report can move a stock ten percent in either direction within a minute. Day traders who try to position before such a release are guessing what the report will say. The professional desks they are competing with often have better tools for the same guess and faster reactions to the actual number.

Flows that have nothing to do with information

A surprising amount of price movement has nothing to do with new information. Index funds rebalance at quarter-end. Pension funds shift between stocks and bonds on a schedule. Options dealers buy and sell the underlying as their hedges shift. Tax-loss selling spikes in December. None of these flows reflect a view about value. They simply move prices because someone has to buy or sell at a particular moment. A retail trader watching the chart often cannot tell the difference between a flow-driven move and a real one.

Stories and narratives

Markets also move because stories take hold. A new technology theme, a geopolitical event, a celebrity endorsement of a stock — these can pull capital toward certain names for months or years. Some narratives turn out to be real (the personal computer, the internet, smartphones). Others fade and leave most of the late entrants with losses. A trader riding a narrative without understanding it tends to enter late, exit late, and pay for the round trip both times.

Order books and microstructure

Underneath all of this is the order book — the list of buy and sell orders waiting to be filled. Big stop-loss clusters above round numbers act like magnets; once price reaches them, the cascade pulls it further. A thin Sunday-evening futures book can turn a small headline into a multi-percent move that fully retraces by Monday morning. Knowing how the plumbing works does not make a trader profitable, but not knowing how it works almost guarantees the opposite.

Why short-term prediction is so hard

Each of these forces operates on a different time scale. Interest-rate shifts play out over months and years. Earnings move single stocks for days. Flows distort prices for hours. Microstructure moves them for seconds. To trade short-term, you have to read several of these at once, in real time, while sized large enough to put real money at risk. The world's best institutions employ teams of specialists to do this and still lose money in many windows.

Retail traders, working alone with one screen and one cup of coffee, are competing against those teams. The result of that mismatch is the failure rate the academic studies keep finding.

What this chapter is not saying

It is not saying you cannot understand what moves prices. The forces above are visible, well documented, and worth learning. It is saying that knowing them at a high level is not the same as predicting their effect on the next thirty-minute candle. The forces are what they are. What changes is which one will dominate in any given moment, and that is the part that almost no one calls correctly in advance, every time, after costs.

How information becomes a price

Most of the time, prices change because someone with new information acts on it. A buyer who knows something you do not is willing to pay a little more, lifts the offer, and the price moves up. A seller in the opposite position pushes it down. Across millions of small decisions, the chart on your screen is the running record of everyone who acted today.

The honest implication is uncomfortable for short-term traders. By the time you see a price move, the people who knew first have already acted. You are reacting to their decisions, not making your own ahead of them. To make money on short moves, you have to either be faster than they are, or know something they do not. Most retail traders, if they are honest, are not faster, and the things they think they know are usually already in the price.

Surprises move prices, not facts

It is not the news itself that moves prices. It is the gap between the news and what was already expected. A company can report record profits and still see its stock fall, because the market was expecting even higher profits. A central bank can raise interest rates and watch bonds rise, because the rate hike was smaller than feared. The gap between expectation and reality is the part that moves.

This makes short-term news trading much harder than it sounds. Knowing what the news will say is not enough. You also have to know what the rest of the market was expecting it to say, before it was said. Professional desks spend enormous resources tracking expectations. Retail traders rarely have a complete picture, which means they often trade the news in the wrong direction.

Liquidity providers and the order book

Behind every visible price is an order book — a list of buy orders waiting to be filled at various prices and sell orders waiting on the other side. Most of those orders come from professional firms whose business is to be on both sides of the market constantly, capturing the spread. They are called market makers or liquidity providers. They do not bet on direction. They bet that they can buy at the bid and sell at the ask faster than the market can move against them.

These firms are not your enemies, but they are not your friends either. Their existence is why a retail trader can buy and sell quickly at all. Their cost is the spread the trader pays each round trip. Understanding that the visible price is being constantly shaped by participants whose only goal is to capture that spread changes how you read a chart. The chart is not a story. It is a residue of professional activity, with retail orders sprinkled in.

Why most short-term forecasts go wrong

Pull these threads together and the difficulty of short-term forecasting becomes clear. The market is responding to a constantly shifting mix of new information, expectation gaps, flow-driven mechanics, and microstructure noise, all interpreted by participants with different time horizons and different goals. A retail trader trying to call the next thirty minutes is trying to read all of those layers at once, in real time, while their own attention is divided and their position is sized in a way that makes calm thinking difficult.

The professionals who do this for a living have teams, tools, and decades of experience. They still get it wrong often. The retail trader has a phone and a coffee. The result of that mismatch is the failure rate the data keeps reporting.

Why economic forecasts almost never help

Every January, financial publications print predictions from professional economists about where markets will go that year. Track those predictions across many years and the result is humbling. The forecasts are right about as often as random chance would suggest. The publications keep printing them anyway, because readers want them, even though following them would have produced no better results than ignoring them.

The lesson is not that forecasting is useless in principle. It is that forecasting twelve months of market behavior, in a system as complex as the global economy, is harder than human judgment can reliably manage. The investor who builds a strategy that depends on economic forecasts is building on sand. The investor who builds a strategy that does not depend on forecasts — diversified, low-cost, patient — is building on something firmer.

How news really arrives

By the time a piece of news reaches the trader on a phone notification, it has already been parsed by professional firms with machine-readable feeds, often before the headline is even formatted for human readers. Their orders have already moved the price. The retail trader looking at the chart in the moments after the news is reacting to a price that has already absorbed the most obvious implications. The remaining moves come from second-order effects — repositioning, hedging, follow-on flows — that are much harder to anticipate.

This means that trading the headline is, for retail, almost always trading after the fact. The honest trader recognizes this and either avoids news-driven trades or sizes them very small, treating them as the lottery tickets they functionally are. The dishonest version is to keep trading the news, lose consistently, and blame the volatility rather than the timing.

Why narrative matters more than fundamentals over short windows

On a long-enough timeline, fundamentals dominate. Earnings, cash flow, and balance-sheet strength eventually show up in prices. Over short windows, however, narrative often dominates. A company can produce excellent earnings and see its stock fall because the prevailing story has shifted to what comes next, not what already happened. A company can produce mediocre earnings and see its stock rise because the narrative has improved. The narrative is not the same as the fundamentals, and the gap between them can persist longer than a short-term trader can stay solvent betting against it.

This is one of the reasons short-term trading is so hard even when the underlying analysis is correct. The trader can be right about the business and wrong about the price for months or years. The patient investor with a longer horizon can wait the gap out. The leveraged short-term trader cannot.

Time horizon is, again, the crucial variable.

Why volatility itself is a feature

Markets are volatile because they aggregate the decisions of millions of participants with different information, different goals, and different time horizons. The volatility is not a bug to be eliminated. It is the natural shape of how prices form when the underlying data is uncertain. A market that did not fluctuate would not be discovering prices; it would be ignoring them.

For a short-term trader, volatility is the friction that costs them money on every round trip. For a long-term investor, the same volatility is the source of their advantage. The long-term investor benefits when fearful sellers push prices down, because their automatic contributions buy more shares. They benefit when overconfident buyers push prices up, because their existing shares are worth more. The same volatility that punishes one approach rewards the other. The difference is the time horizon.

Why interest rates are the silent center

Among all the factors that move prices, interest rates set by central banks are the most consistently powerful. They affect the price of money itself, which affects the price of every asset that competes with money for capital. When rates rise, the present value of future cash flows falls, and the prices of stocks, bonds, and most other assets adjust downward to reflect it. When rates fall, the opposite happens.

This is not a theory. It is the mechanical consequence of how present-value calculations work. A trader or investor who does not understand this relationship is missing one of the few reliable structural forces in the market. The retail trader who tries to predict short-term rate moves usually loses to professional desks with better information. The patient investor who simply accepts that rates will go up sometimes and down sometimes, and holds a diversified portfolio across the cycle, captures whatever the cycle eventually delivers without having to forecast it.

Chapter 6

Crypto Currency Market

Cryptocurrencies arrived as a technology promise: digital money that does not need a central bank, a public ledger that does not need a single owner, programmable contracts that run on their own. Some of that promise is real and interesting. Whether the financial instruments built on top of it are appropriate for ordinary people to day trade is a different question, with a much harder answer.

What makes crypto different

Crypto markets share most of the disadvantages of every other day-trading market and add a few of their own. They trade twenty-four hours a day, seven days a week. There is no closing bell, which sounds like opportunity but mostly means the trader is either watching a screen at all hours or missing moves while asleep. Liquidity is split across hundreds of venues with no single tape, so the same coin can trade at meaningfully different prices on different exchanges, especially during stress.

Volatility is much higher than in traditional markets. Even the largest coins have produced drawdowns of seventy or eighty percent within a year, then recovered, then done it again. That is not a defect being slowly fixed. That has been the pattern for more than a decade.

Where do you actually keep it

Owning a coin is not like owning shares in a brokerage account. There is no government insurance equivalent to FDIC for bank deposits or SIPC for U.S. brokerages. You can hold coins on a centralized exchange, which is convenient but means you are trusting that exchange to stay solvent and honest. The history is not reassuring. A long list of exchanges has frozen withdrawals, gone bankrupt, or simply disappeared with customer funds. When that happens, the customer becomes an unsecured claim in a bankruptcy, and recovery — if it comes at all — takes years.

The alternative is self-custody: holding the coins in a wallet whose secret keys you control. That removes the exchange risk and adds an operational one. Lose the keys, lose the coins. Get the wallet stolen, lose the coins. Send to the wrong address, lose the coins. Both options carry real risk, just different shapes of it.

Manipulation is normal here

Pump-and-dump schemes are a routine feature of crypto markets, not an exception. A small group buys a token cheaply, pushes a story across social media, sells into the resulting demand, and moves on. The lifecycle takes days or weeks. The chart looks like a moonshot followed by a cliff. Most of the buyers who arrived after the social-media wave are holding the cliff.

On decentralized exchanges, there is also "maximal extractable value," which is a clean-sounding term for validators reordering transactions inside a block to capture a slice of every trade that passes through. A retail trader executing a large swap on one of these venues without protection regularly pays a hidden cost on top of the visible fee.

The case for a small allocation

There is a defensible argument for owning a small amount of bitcoin, ether, or both as a long-term position inside a diversified portfolio — sized so that if it goes to zero, your life does not change. That is investing, in the patient sense of the word, not day trading. The volatility of these assets does not reward short-term speculation by retail traders any more than it does in stocks. It just reaches its punishing conclusions faster.

Day trading crypto specifically

Crypto day trading combines all the difficulties of equity day trading with weaker custody, less regulation, more leverage at offshore venues, and more outright fraud at the smaller end of the market. None of that is fixable by a better chart program. A trader who would not feel comfortable handing the family savings to a stranger should not feel comfortable handing it to most crypto exchanges, either.

The next chapter looks at the two main toolkits day traders use to make decisions — technical analysis and fundamental analysis — and at where each one helps and where each one misleads.

What changes when there is no closing bell

Stock markets close. Their hours give traders breaks, force decisions to be deferred to the next session, and concentrate liquidity into known windows. Crypto has none of that. The market runs all day, every day. A trader who tries to follow it the way they would follow the U.S. equity session ends up either watching screens at strange hours or missing significant moves while sleeping.

The continuous nature of crypto sounds like opportunity. In practice, it is mostly fatigue. A market that never closes is a market that never gives the trader's nervous system a chance to rest. Decisions made at 3 a.m. on a small phone screen are not better decisions. They are simply later ones.

Why exchanges are not banks

When you deposit money in a bank, it is insured by the government up to a limit. If the bank fails, you get your money back. When you deposit money or coins in a crypto exchange, there is generally no equivalent protection. If the exchange fails — and many have — your balance becomes a claim in a bankruptcy proceeding that may take years to resolve, and may resolve at a fraction of what you were owed.

This is not a theoretical concern. Several large exchanges have collapsed in recent years, taking billions of dollars in customer balances with them. The lesson is not to avoid crypto entirely. The lesson is to understand what you actually own when you hold coins on an exchange. You own a promise from a private company that may or may not be solvent. That is a different thing from owning the coins themselves.

The hidden costs of trading on-chain

Decentralized exchanges run on blockchains that charge fees for every action. These fees are sometimes small and sometimes substantial, depending on the network's congestion. A trade that looks profitable on the screen can become a loss after the network fee is paid, especially for small positions.

There is also a less obvious cost called maximal extractable value, where the participants who order transactions inside each block can rearrange them to capture spread from the trades they include. The retail user who places a large swap on a decentralized exchange without protection often pays an invisible tax on top of the visible fee. This is not a scam in the traditional sense; it is built into how some blockchains work. But it is a real cost, and most retail crypto traders have never heard of it.

The honest case for owning a little

There is a defensible argument for owning a small amount of bitcoin or ether — the two largest and most established coins — as part of a diversified long-term portfolio. The size should be small enough that a complete loss would not affect your life. The purpose is to have some exposure to a new technology category that may, or may not, prove durable across decades.

That argument is for investing, not for day trading. Owning a coin for years is a different activity from buying it in the morning and trying to sell it for more by lunch. The volatility that makes bitcoin interesting as a long-term experiment makes it punishing as a short-term trade. The same daily swings that produce occasional dramatic gains produce equally dramatic losses, and the trader has to time both correctly to come out ahead. Almost no one does that consistently.

Why volatility means short-term outcomes are random

Bitcoin's daily volatility, even in calm regimes, is several times that of major stock indices. In stressed regimes, it is much higher. What this means for a short-term trader is that the signal-to-noise ratio is poor. A real edge — a strategy that, on average, makes a small amount of money per trade — gets buried in the random noise of daily moves that have nothing to do with the strategy.

Imagine a coin that on average rises a quarter of a percent per day. Over a year, that compounds to a substantial return. Inside any given day, however, the actual move can range from minus ten percent to plus ten percent. The trader who guesses correctly which day will deliver which move can do well; the trader who guesses incorrectly does poorly; and the average retail trader, guessing roughly fifty-fifty, ends up being eaten by transaction costs while the underlying coin grinds slowly higher in the background. Holding patiently captures the slow grind. Short-term trading does not.

What "not your keys, not your coins" actually means

The crypto community has a slogan: not your keys, not your coins. It means that if the cryptographic keys to a wallet are not in your direct control, you do not actually own the coins inside it. You own a promise from whoever holds the keys — usually an exchange — that they will let you withdraw the coins when you ask. Most of the time, the promise is honored. Sometimes, the exchange fails, freezes withdrawals, or vanishes, and the customer who thought they owned coins discovers they owned an unsecured claim against a bankrupt company.

The alternative — self-custody, where you hold the keys yourself — eliminates the exchange-failure risk and adds operational risk. You can lose the keys. You can be socially engineered out of them. You can send to the wrong address. Both options carry real risk, just different shapes. A reader holding any meaningful amount of crypto should understand which form of risk they are accepting and why.

What "decentralized" really delivers

Decentralization is a core marketing claim of crypto. The promise is that no single party controls the system, no one can freeze your assets, no government can confiscate them. In some narrow respects, this is true: a coin held in self-custody, with private keys you control, is hard for any third party to seize. The claim is also misleading in some important ways.

The decentralized system still depends on infrastructure that is not equally distributed: a small number of large exchanges where most trading happens, a small number of mining or validation pools that produce most blocks, a small number of stablecoin issuers whose decisions affect billions of dollars of activity. When something goes wrong — an exchange fails, a stablecoin de-pegs, a major protocol is exploited — the harm flows through these centralized choke points the same way it would in traditional finance. The decentralization is partial and conditional. Anyone evaluating the claim should look at where the actual power and money sit, not just at the marketing language.

Why exchanges keep failing

The pattern of crypto exchange failures is depressingly consistent. An exchange grows quickly during a market boom, expands aggressively, becomes a major venue for retail and institutional flow. Then a stress event arrives — a price decline, a regulatory action, a security breach. Customer withdrawals spike. The exchange discovers it does not have the reserves it claimed. It freezes withdrawals. Within weeks, it files for bankruptcy. Customers learn that their balances were not actually segregated, were not insured, and may take years to partially recover, if at all.

Each major failure produces public commitments from other exchanges that they would never operate this way. Some of those commitments are sincere and supported by actual reserve audits. Some are not. The reader holding funds on any exchange should know which kind of exchange they are dealing with. The information is partial — full transparency does not exist in this industry — but partial information is better than the assumption that all exchanges are safe because they have not failed yet. Any exchange can fail. Many have. The next one might.

Why crypto enthusiasm and crypto investment are different things

It is possible to be enthusiastic about cryptocurrency as a technology while being cautious about it as an investment. The two questions are different. The technology may, or may not, prove durable across decades; that is a question about cryptography, software, and adoption. The investment value of any specific token at the current price is a question about supply, demand, and what the market is willing to pay tomorrow.

A reader who finds the technology interesting can support it in many ways without necessarily holding speculative positions. They can use the products. They can read about the developments. They can hold a small position sized as a speculation, walled off from real savings. None of these activities require them to bet large amounts of household wealth on which token will rise next. The conflation of "believing in the technology" with "holding the token" is a marketing trick. The two are separable, and the reader who keeps them separate makes calmer decisions.

Custody habits worth keeping

If you hold any meaningful amount of cryptocurrency, a few small habits reduce a large amount of risk. Keep amounts you are not actively trading off of exchanges, in a hardware wallet whose recovery phrase is written down (not stored on a phone or computer) and kept somewhere safe. Spread holdings across more than one location if the total is large enough to justify the operational effort. Treat seed phrases the way you would treat the deed to a house. Test recovery procedures occasionally on small amounts so that, if you ever need them at scale, you know they work.

These habits feel paranoid until they save you. The reader who has lost coins to an exchange failure, a phishing attack, or a forgotten password will tell you that the operational care was worth several times what it cost. The reader who has never lost coins might assume the care is unnecessary, until the day it would have been necessary. The asymmetry favors caution.

Chapter 7

Technical and Fundamental Analysis

Two different ways of trying to understand a security have grown up alongside each other. They are usually presented as rival camps. They are better understood as different tools, useful for different questions, each with real strengths and real limits.

Technical analysis in plain words

Technical analysis is the study of price and volume. The technical analyst looks at charts, draws lines on them, computes indicators (moving averages, oscillators, volume studies), and tries to spot patterns that have, in the past, been followed by certain kinds of moves. The reasoning is that price reflects the actions of all participants, including those who know more, and that aggregate behavior leaves footprints in the chart.

There is some truth to it. Trends do exist. Momentum effects have been documented in research. Mean-reversion exists in some markets some of the time. But the share of technical material being sold to retail traders that has any statistical evidence behind it is small. Most of the patterns in the books are pattern-matched after the fact: the cases where they worked are remembered; the cases where they did not are forgotten.

Fundamental analysis in plain words

Fundamental analysis tries to estimate what a business is actually worth, then compares that estimate to the price the market is asking. The analyst looks at revenue, profit margins, growth rate, debt, return on capital, the durability of the business, the quality of the people running it. The output is a rough estimate of intrinsic value. The decision is to buy when the price is meaningfully below that estimate and to walk away (or sell) when it is well above it.

Fundamental analysis is what real investors do. It is also harder than it sounds. The inputs are uncertain — every estimate of the future depends on assumptions that may be wrong. Industries can be disrupted by changes that no spreadsheet captured. The analyst's own opinion can shape the answer if they are not careful.

Which one suits which time frame

Time horizon matters. Fundamental analysis is a long-term tool. The information advantages it produces play out over years, not minutes. If you build a careful model of a business and the price is below your estimate of its value, the market does not have to agree with you tomorrow. It often does not. Patient capital can wait. Day-trading capital cannot.

Technical analysis is sometimes useful for shorter time frames, but only modestly so, and only after costs are accounted for. Many "setups" produce small gross edges that disappear once the spread, slippage, and short-term tax friction are subtracted. The genuine technical edges that survive are usually subtle, statistical, and exploited by professional firms running them at scale.

Where retail traders typically go wrong

The most common mistake is to treat charts as if they could replace business analysis. A pattern on a five-minute chart of a small company tells you nothing about whether the company will exist in five years. The trader who buys on the pattern and ignores the company is hoping the price is the truth. It is not. The price is the latest opinion of millions of participants, many of whom know less about the company than you could learn in a single afternoon of careful reading.

The mirror mistake is to ignore price discipline because the fundamentals look strong. Even a good business can be a bad investment at a high enough price. The patient investor needs both: a sense of what the business is worth and a willingness to wait until the price meets that sense.

What works in practice

For the patient investor described in the previous chapter, fundamentals come first and price discipline comes second. The simplest version is to skip individual analysis altogether and own the whole market through a low-cost index fund. The more advanced version is to own a small number of businesses you understand at prices that leave room for being wrong.

For the active trader, the most useful thing technical analysis can do is keep you on the right side of obvious trends and away from obvious traps. It is not a magic recipe. The next two chapters look at the limits of each toolkit in more detail, starting with fundamental analysis.

How professionals actually use these tools

It helps to know what serious institutional analysts actually do, because what they do is different from what is taught in retail courses. Professional fundamental analysts spend most of their time reading. Annual reports, quarterly filings, conference call transcripts, industry trade publications, customer interviews, supplier interviews. The financial model they eventually build is the smallest part of the work. The reading is what produces the judgment.

Professional technical analysts, where they exist, are usually quantitative researchers running statistical tests on large datasets. They are not drawing trend lines on a daily chart. They are testing whether a measurable property of past prices predicts future prices, in a sample large enough to distinguish skill from luck, and whether the predicted edge survives realistic transaction costs. Most of their tested ideas do not work.

What is sold to retail traders as "fundamental analysis" is usually a quick read of recent earnings, with no real understanding of the business. What is sold as "technical analysis" is usually pattern recognition by the human eye, which the brain does poorly under uncertainty. The retail versions of both methods are watered-down imitations of the professional ones, with most of the difficult work removed.

The honest case for each tool

Fundamental analysis, used carefully, helps a long-term investor decide which businesses are worth owning at which prices. It is slow, requires real reading, and usually points to fewer purchases than the investor would otherwise make. That is a feature, not a bug. The patient investor who owns ten carefully chosen businesses for a decade tends to do better than the impatient one who owns fifty for six months each.

Technical analysis, used modestly, can help any market participant avoid the most obvious traps. A simple rule like "do not add to a stock that has been declining for months" is technical analysis. It is also common sense. Where technical tools earn their keep is in helping you stay on the right side of obvious trends and out of obvious blowups. Where they fail is in promising more — that they can predict short-term moves with enough reliability to overcome trading costs. They cannot.

Combining the two without fooling yourself

Some of the most successful long-term investors use a combination of both tools. They identify businesses worth owning through fundamental analysis. They use simple technical filters to avoid buying into obvious downtrends. They hold for years. They rarely sell. The combination works because each tool is being used for what it is good at — fundamentals for choosing what to own, technicals as a small sanity check on timing — and neither is asked to do something it cannot do.

The retail trader who uses both tools to make minute-by-minute decisions is not getting the benefit of either. They are using the wrong tool at the wrong time scale, paying full transaction costs every round trip, and producing a track record that almost guarantees losses after costs.

What a quality business looks like

Plain-English markers of a quality business, the kind a fundamental investor pays attention to: the business produces cash flows that are growing, not just revenues. It has more revenue today than five years ago, and meaningfully more cash flow. It can raise prices on its customers without losing them. It does not require constant heavy investment just to stay in place. It has paid down debt or grown without taking on much. Its management owns substantial stock and acts like owners.

These markers do not require sophisticated analysis. They require reading a few annual reports, looking at five years of numbers, and asking whether what you see matches what the management says about itself. Most retail investors who try this for the first time discover that some companies they thought were great look mediocre on the numbers, and some companies they had ignored look much better. The numbers are not magic. They are just a calmer source of information than the daily news.

What charts can and cannot tell you

A chart shows what happened. That is all. It does not show why something happened. It does not show what is about to happen. It does not show what the underlying business is doing or whether the company is healthy. The trader who treats the chart as a complete picture is treating effect as cause.

Used modestly, a chart can confirm or filter a decision made for other reasons. If you have read the company's reports and concluded the business is in trouble, but the stock keeps making new highs, the chart is information — perhaps the market knows something you do not. If your business analysis says a stock is attractively priced and the chart shows it has been declining steadily for months, the chart is also information — perhaps you are early. Used as the only input, the chart is a story dressed up as an answer. Used as one input among several, it can be useful.

What patient investors actually use

Patient long-term investors typically use a small subset of fundamental tools and almost no technical tools. They look at a company's revenue and profit growth over five to ten years. They check the balance sheet for excessive debt. They read the management's letters to shareholders to get a sense of whether management thinks like owners or like employees. They estimate whether the business has a durable advantage that protects it from competition. They compare the current price to a rough estimate of intrinsic value, and they buy when there is a meaningful discount and refuse to buy when there is not.

None of this requires advanced training. It requires patience, willingness to read, and the discipline to wait for opportunities rather than forcing them. A reader who does this much, on a small number of well-chosen businesses, will likely do better over decades than the average professional money manager and dramatically better than the average retail trader. The unglamorous tools are the ones that work.

Why simple beats complex over time

There is a tendency in financial education to associate sophistication with good results. More indicators must be better than fewer. More models must be better than one. More inputs must be better than ten. The empirical record disagrees. Across decades of research on professional fund management, simpler approaches have generally outperformed complex ones, after costs.

The reason is partly that complexity creates more opportunities for error and partly that complex systems often optimize for the past rather than for any reliable future. A simple approach — own a diversified set of productive businesses, contribute regularly, hold for decades — does not require getting many things right. A complex approach requires getting many things right, and small mistakes in any of them compound into large differences in outcome. For most investors, the simpler version is not just easier to execute; it is also more likely to produce the result the complex version was supposed to deliver.

Why a checklist beats a feeling

Both fundamental and technical analysis benefit from being reduced to checklists, when possible. A fundamental checklist might ask: revenue and earnings growing for five years, manageable debt, durable competitive advantage, honest management, reasonable price relative to estimated value. A technical checklist might ask: above the long-term moving average, no obvious distribution pattern, volume confirming recent moves. Each item is yes or no. The decision flows from the checklist.

Checklists feel mechanical. They are. The point of mechanical processes is that they do not depend on the trader feeling clever in the moment. They produce consistent decisions even when the trader is tired, stressed, or excited about something irrelevant. Across decades, mechanical processes outperform expert judgment in many domains, including investing. The investor who follows a simple checklist wlll likely outperform the investor who relies on intuition, even if the intuitive investor sometimes feels they have insight the checklist would have missed.

Chapter 8

Fundamental Analysis Risks

Fundamental analysis is the better of the two retail tools for thinking about value, but it is not a guarantee. Used carelessly, it produces confidence without protection. Used in isolation from price discipline, it leads to overpaying for businesses that are good but not good enough at the price quoted. This chapter walks through the most common ways it goes wrong.

Forecasts are guesses

Every valuation, however careful, contains a forecast. Future revenue, future margins, future investment needs, future cost of capital — all of them have to be estimated. Small changes to long-term assumptions can swing the result by enormous percentages. A two-percentage-point change in assumed long-term growth rate, used in a typical model, can double or halve the answer. Anyone who shows you a single point estimate is hiding the fragility of the math underneath. Honest practitioners produce a range and tell you where they sit inside it.

The numbers can lie politely

Reported financial statements are accurate within the rules of accounting, and those rules leave plenty of room for choice. Companies decide when to recognize revenue, what to count as an investment versus an expense, how to value inventory, what assumptions to use for pension liabilities. Most management teams play these choices honestly. Some do not. Even among honest ones, a single quarter's numbers blend real operating results with accounting decisions that can mask or amplify them.

Industry-specific quirks matter too. A subscription software company should be analyzed differently from a bank or an oil producer. A general-purpose investor who applies the same metrics to every business will reach the wrong answer in industries they do not understand.

The world keeps changing

The most expensive fundamental mistakes come from being right about today's math and wrong about tomorrow's world. A company can have strong margins, a wide moat, and excellent management and still be eroded by a technology shift the analyst did not see coming. The history of value investing is full of textile mills, video stores, retail chains, and printer-cartridge businesses that looked cheap on every conventional measure right before structural decline accelerated.

The defense is not to predict every disruption. Almost no one does that well. The defense is to demand a wide enough margin between price and value that being wrong about the future does not destroy the investment.

The analyst is a human being

Once you have done substantial work on a company, you become attached to the conclusion. New information that supports the thesis is welcomed; new information that contradicts it gets explained away. This is not a flaw in any one person. It is how human cognition works. The defenses are practical: write the thesis down, write the conditions under which you would change your mind, and review periodically with someone who has no stake in the answer.

Value can be wrong forever

A patient analyst can spot a stock trading below fair value and watch it sit there for years. The market does not have to agree with you, and the longer it disagrees, the more the time value of money works against you. Real value investors accept this. They size positions so they can wait out long disagreements without being forced to sell. They also accept that some of their best ideas will simply never work, because the world will change before the market notices.

Why this matters for day traders

Day traders sometimes layer light fundamental research on top of intraday charts. They read a few lines about the company, decide it is "a good business," and then trade five-minute candles around earnings. This is using a long-range telescope to read a street sign. Fundamentals are about years. Intraday price action is about minutes. There is no realistic mechanism by which a careful estimate of a business's value tells you what the next thirty minutes will do.

Used well, fundamental analysis is the foundation of patient investing. Used as window dressing on short-term trading, it adds confidence without adding edge. The next chapter looks at the same problem from the technical side.

What a moat actually is

When fundamental analysts talk about a business having a "moat," they mean some durable advantage that makes it hard for competitors to take its market. The most common moats are network effects, where the product gets better as more people use it; switching costs, where it would be expensive or annoying for customers to leave; intangible assets like a brand or a regulatory license; cost advantages from scale; and what is called efficient scale, where the market is just large enough to support a few players profitably.

A wide moat is the closest thing to a guarantee that a long-term investor can find. A narrow moat is more fragile. No moat at all means the business is exposed to whatever competitors decide to do, and competitors usually decide to do the most painful thing. The skill of identifying which moats are real, and which are claimed but not real, is the heart of long-term equity investing. It is also harder than it looks, because a lot of mediocre businesses describe themselves as having moats they do not actually have.

The graveyard of cheap stocks

Value investing — buying things that look cheap on the numbers — sounds simple. The historical record contains a long list of stocks that looked cheap on every reasonable measure right before they got a lot cheaper. Sometimes the cheapness was a signal that something was wrong with the business. Sometimes the world changed in a way the model did not predict. Sometimes the management was less honest than the financial statements suggested.

The defense against this is not better forecasting. It is wider margins of safety, smaller positions in any single name, and willingness to walk away from ideas when new information shows that the original case was wrong. Real value investors are not stubborn. They have strong opinions, weakly held, and they are honest with themselves when the evidence shifts.

When fundamental analysis is most useful

Fundamental analysis is most useful at long time horizons. It tells you, with reasonable confidence, that a business is worth somewhere in a range. It does not tell you what the price will do next week. The longer you hold, the more the underlying economics show up in the price, and the less it matters that you bought a few percent above or below your estimate of fair value.

This is why fundamental analysis is the foundation of patient investing and an unhelpful add-on for day trading. The analyst is using a long-range tool to answer a short-range question. The tool was not designed for that, and it does not perform well there.

The two-question test

Before buying any individual stock, two simple questions are worth answering honestly. First: do you understand how this business actually makes money? Not the press-release version, the real version. If you cannot explain it to a curious twelve-year-old in two minutes, you do not understand it well enough yet. Second: would you be comfortable holding the stock for five years, even if its price did not change at all in that period? If the answer is no, you are buying for the price move, not for the business.

Most retail purchases of individual stocks fail one or both questions. The investor knows the company name, but not the actual economics. They are buying because they expect a price move, not because they want to be a long-term part-owner. Both failures point in the same direction: the purchase is closer to speculation than to investment, and the right size for a speculative position is a small fraction of household assets, not a large bet.

Why analyst ratings are mostly noise

Wall Street analysts publish ratings — buy, hold, sell — on individual stocks. Television and newspapers report changes in those ratings as if they were meaningful. Track the ratings honestly, however, and most of the meaning disappears. The vast majority of analyst ratings are buy or hold; sell ratings are rare and often issued well after the stock has already declined. The ratings reflect the analyst's career incentives — being too bearish on a covered company can cost them access — at least as much as their honest view.

This is not an argument that all analysts are dishonest. Many are thoughtful and write useful research. The argument is that the published rating is one of the least informative parts of analyst output. The detailed reasoning behind it, where it is available, is more useful than the rating itself. A retail investor reading a research report should focus on the analysis and ignore the buy/hold/sell label.

When the moat actually erodes

The hardest fundamental mistake to recognize in real time is moat erosion. A business that has dominated its market for decades can find that the dominance is slowly being eaten away — by a competitor that does the same thing slightly better, by a technology shift that reduces the importance of what the business is good at, or by changing customer preferences that the management did not see soon enough. Each year looks fine on the numbers. The cumulative drift, over a decade, can be devastating.

The defenses are imperfect but real. Pay attention to whether competitors are gaining ground year over year. Read trade publications, not just the company's own materials, because management is rarely the first to announce that the moat is shrinking. Pay attention to capital expenditures: a moat that requires more and more investment to maintain is a moat that may not be holding. The patient investor who watches for these signals can usually exit a deteriorating business before the deterioration shows up in obvious ways. The investor who only looks at the past five years of numbers, and never the qualitative signals, often gets caught.

When honest people disagree about value

Two careful fundamental analysts can look at the same business and arrive at meaningfully different estimates of intrinsic value. They are not making errors. They are making different judgments about future growth, future capital needs, future competitive dynamics. The honest answer to "what is this business worth?" is usually a range, not a number, and the range can be wide enough that two thoughtful investors reach different practical decisions.

This is uncomfortable for readers who want certainty. The honest investor learns to live with the discomfort. The investor who insists on a single answer often gets it by ignoring the inputs that make the answer uncertain, which is how confident wrong opinions are formed. The investor who acknowledges the range buys when the price is below even the conservative end of the range, refuses to buy when the price is above the optimistic end, and accepts the cases in between as ambiguous and not worth strong action. This is slower than the certain version. It is also more accurate, on the whole.

Why management quality matters most

Among all the inputs to fundamental analysis, management quality is the hardest to measure and one of the most important to get right. A great business with poor management can deteriorate slowly into a mediocre one. A mediocre business with great management can be rebuilt into something durable. The financial statements show the past. Management decides the future.

Reading the management's annual letters to shareholders, across multiple years, is one of the cheapest ways to evaluate this. Honest management writes plainly, takes responsibility for mistakes, explains decisions in terms of long-term value, and provides specific operating metrics that hold up over time. Less honest management writes vaguely, blames external factors, emphasizes adjusted earnings that consistently differ from real ones, and shifts metrics whenever the previously emphasized one stops looking favorable. The contrast is visible after reading a few letters in sequence. It is also one of the strongest predictors of long-term outcomes for investors who pay attention to it.

Chapter 9

Technical Analysis Risks

If fundamental analysis can fail because the world surprises the model, technical analysis can fail because the model itself was never very strong to begin with. This chapter is not a blanket dismissal — there are real, documented effects in price data — but a careful list of why most of what is sold as technical analysis to retail traders does not survive realistic costs and basic statistical scrutiny.

Lots of patterns work — by chance

Imagine running ten thousand made-up trading rules across the historical price of any actively traded stock. Purely by luck, hundreds of them will look profitable on past data. The marketing pipeline that surrounds technical analysis is built around showing the winners and forgetting the rest. When a course or a video says "this setup is right seventy-eight percent of the time," it was almost always selected from a much larger pool of setups that did not work.

Curve-fitting and backtesting

A rule with enough adjustable parameters can fit any past chart almost perfectly. The same rule, applied to data the rule has not seen yet, usually performs no better than coin flips. Honest backtesting requires what professionals call walk-forward testing, plus realistic transaction costs, plus out-of-sample data. Almost no retail course on technical analysis enforces any of those.

Even real edges are small

Even the technical effects that survive academic scrutiny are small in retail terms. A rule that produces a positive expected value of a few tenths of a percent per trade looks promising until the spread, slippage, and short-term tax bite are subtracted. What remains is often a coin flip with extra clicks. The professionals who do exploit small edges do so at scale, with expensive infrastructure and tight cost control. None of that is replicable on a phone.

The brain finds patterns that are not there

Humans are wired to spot patterns. We see faces in clouds, animals in tea leaves, and head-and-shoulders formations in random walks. Studies have shown that experienced chart readers identify just as many "valid" patterns in artificially generated noise as they do in real price data. Pattern recognition feels like skill. It is sometimes skill, but it is often the brain doing what brains do.

Indicators repeat themselves

Most popular indicators — RSI, MACD, stochastics, moving averages — are different mathematical transformations of the same underlying price data. Stacking three or four of them on a chart and waiting for them to "agree" is not adding independent confirmation. It is dressing up the same signal as several signals and feeling more confident than the evidence justifies.

Markets change regimes

An indicator that worked beautifully through one period can stop working in the next. Mean-reversion strategies thrive in choppy markets and bleed in trending ones. Trend-following thrives in clean directional moves and breaks down in choppy years. The trader who learned a system in one regime and assumes it will keep working is in for an expensive education when the regime changes.

When too many people see the same pattern

Once everyone knows the same setup, the setup stops working. Stops above resistance and below support become magnets that algorithmic traders use against the crowd. Breakouts above obvious levels get faded. The textbook patterns that worked when only the textbook readers saw them stop working when the textbook is on every trading channel on the internet.

Where technical tools earn their keep

Used modestly, technical tools have legitimate uses. A simple moving-average filter can keep a long-term investor from buying an entire portfolio of stocks while the broad market is in obvious decline. Volume analysis can flag when a move lacks conviction. Trend confirmation can keep a trader from fighting an obvious tape. These are minor, supporting roles. They are not the replacements for thinking that retail courses present them as.

> *If a chart pattern were as reliable as advertised, the people teaching it would be on a beach, not on a livestream selling courses.*

The next chapter steps away from the tools and looks at the part of the trader the tools are supposed to help: the human mind under pressure.

Why most patterns are not patterns

The human brain is built to find patterns. We see faces in clouds. We hear voices in static. We spot head-and-shoulders formations in random charts. Researchers have shown that experienced traders, given charts of pure noise dressed up to look like price data, identify just as many "valid" patterns as they do in real markets. Pattern recognition feels like skill, and sometimes it is, but most of the time it is the brain doing what brains do.

This is not an argument that no pattern is ever real. Some statistical patterns in markets are documented and survive testing. The argument is that the patterns sold in retail courses are usually selected from a much larger pool of failed patterns, by survivorship bias, and that the brain confirms them eagerly because the brain confirms most things eagerly. A trader who uses patterns honestly has to apply skepticism the brain does not apply on its own.

How to test a pattern honestly

If you genuinely want to know whether a technical pattern works, the test is straightforward to describe and difficult to do. Define the pattern precisely enough that a computer can identify it. Apply it to a long historical data set the rule has never seen. Include realistic transaction costs. Apply the same rule to a separate data set held back from the original test, to make sure the rule was not tuned to the first one. If the rule still produces a meaningful edge after all of that, you may have something.

Almost no one does this. The retail courses that sell technical analysis do not do it. Even most paid newsletters do not. Without honest testing, the rules being taught are stories, not strategies. Some of the stories are entertaining. None of them are reliable enough to overcome the transaction costs of active trading.

Where technical analysis is genuinely useful

Used at long time horizons and in modest doses, technical analysis can do a few useful things. It can keep a long-term investor from buying into an obvious decline. It can flag that volume on a move is unusually thin, suggesting the move may not last. It can confirm that a long-term trend is intact before adding to a position. None of these uses involve predicting the next thirty minutes. All of them involve confirming or filtering decisions made for other reasons.

The mistake retail traders make is to treat technical analysis as the primary decision-making tool rather than as a small filter. Once it is the primary tool, the trader is looking at lines on a screen and pretending the lines tell them what is going to happen. They do not.

What a real research process looks like

It is worth contrasting how technical analysis is taught in retail courses with how quantitative researchers actually test trading rules at professional firms. The professional process: define the rule precisely. Apply it to historical data, ideally going back decades. Include realistic transaction costs, market impact, and slippage. Test on out-of-sample data — periods the rule was not developed against. Test on multiple markets to see whether the edge generalizes. Compute statistical significance using methods appropriate for time-series data. Stress-test under different regimes. Refuse to deploy until the evidence is robust.

Most professional ideas, evaluated this way, fail. The few that survive get deployed cautiously, with small position sizes, and are monitored closely for evidence that the edge is decaying. Retail technical analysis, by contrast, is usually presented as if all of those steps had been done and confirmed, when in fact none of them have. The contrast explains a lot of what goes wrong when retail traders apply patterns they read about in courses to their own accounts.

The illusion of confirmation

Stack three or four technical indicators on a chart and wait for them to agree, and you will feel more confident in the resulting trades. The confidence is largely illusory. Most popular indicators are different mathematical transformations of the same underlying price data. RSI, MACD, stochastics, moving averages — they share most of their inputs. When they agree, they are not providing independent confirmation. They are just describing the same recent price action in different ways.

Real confirmation would require independent sources of information: a fundamental thesis, an unrelated quantitative signal, a different market with the same theme. The retail version of confirmation, where multiple chart-based indicators line up, looks like agreement but is mostly redundancy. The trader who takes a position on "three indicators agree" is taking the same trade three times, not three different trades that point the same way.

What the most useful indicator actually does

Among the dozens of popular technical indicators, the most useful one for patient long-term investors is also one of the simplest: a long-term moving average, calculated over many months. A stock or index trading above its long-term moving average is in a long-term uptrend. One trading below it is in a long-term downtrend. The signal is crude. It is also reliable enough to keep a long-term investor from buying into broad declines and to confirm that long-term uptrends are intact.

This is not a trading signal. The investor still needs a real reason to buy, based on what they own and at what price. The moving average is a sanity check, not a decision. Used this way, in modest doses, technical analysis adds something useful. Used as the primary decision tool on short time frames, it overpromises and consistently underdelivers.

Why even tested patterns decay

Suppose you have honestly tested a technical pattern across decades of data, with realistic costs, and the test shows a small positive expected value. Congratulations: you have found something rare. Unfortunately, the very fact that the pattern works tends to make it stop working. Other participants discover similar patterns. They trade ahead of them. The price action that used to follow the pattern stops happening because the trades that would have produced it are now happening earlier.

This is called edge decay, and it is one of the most reliable features of technical analysis at scale. Patterns that worked in the 1990s often stopped working by the 2010s. Patterns that worked in the 2010s are decaying now. The trader who finds a working pattern, deploys it, and assumes it will keep working forever is not paying attention to how markets adapt. The honest practitioner monitors continuously and is willing to retire any pattern that stops producing the expected results.

Why noise looks like signal

On any chart, there are always patterns visible to the human eye. The brain is exceptionally good at finding them. The brain is much worse at telling the difference between patterns that reflect real underlying structure and patterns that are simply random arrangements of price points. This is not a personal failing; it is how human pattern recognition works. The brain evolved to detect predators in tall grass, not to evaluate statistical significance in time-series data.

The honest technician acknowledges this and applies skepticism the brain does not apply on its own. Before trading on a pattern, they ask: would the same pattern be visible in randomly generated data? Has this pattern been tested across decades, with realistic costs, and produced a meaningful edge? Are the wins from the pattern documented in advance, or are they identified only in hindsight? Most retail technical analysis fails these questions. The patterns being traded are stories the brain tells, not statistical features the data supports.

Chapter 10

Role and Risks of Human Emotions

A trader's strategy lives on paper. The trader's decisions live in a body that is tired, scared, hopeful, hungry, and connected to a phone that beeps every two minutes. Decades of research in psychology have catalogued the specific ways in which the human mind misjudges risk under uncertainty. Almost every one of those biases is a hidden tax on day trading. Knowing them does not protect you from them. Understanding them is the first step toward building a system that does.

Loss hurts more than gain feels good

Researchers measure it carefully: the pain of losing a given amount of money is roughly twice as strong as the pleasure of gaining the same amount. The trader's behavior reflects this. Small profits get taken quickly to lock in the good feeling. Losses get held in the hope they will come back. The result is a portfolio of small wins and large losses — exactly the wrong distribution to survive in markets.

Most traders think they are above average

Survey almost any group of drivers and most will rate themselves above average. Survey traders and the same thing happens. The cost is real. Studies of brokerage accounts have found that the most active traders underperform the least active ones by several percentage points per year, and the gap is driven mostly by costs incurred while expressing overconfidence. The lesson is unflattering: trade less, do better.

We see what we expected to see

Once a position is open, the trader unconsciously seeks information that supports the trade and discounts information that contradicts it. The same news headline reads as bullish to a long and bearish to a short. A trading journal, when one exists, often records the trader's story rather than the actual outcome. Writing down the thesis and the conditions under which you would change your mind, before opening the trade, is a small act of discipline that protects against this in real time.

Recent events feel more representative

After a string of wins, the trader expects more wins and sizes up. After a string of losses, fear dominates and the trader sits out the eventual rebound. Both reactions are exactly the opposite of what an honest strategy would do. Position sizes that depend on recent results are usually doing the wrong thing at the wrong time.

We sell winners too early and hold losers too long

The combination of loss aversion and a desire to feel correct produces what researchers call the disposition effect. Traders close winners early to bank a small certain gain and hold losers in the hope they will recover. Tax considerations actually run the opposite way — short-term losses are useful, short-term gains are penalized — but emotional accounting wins over rational tax planning in real-time decisions.

Hindsight rewrites the chart

After the fact, every market move feels obvious. The trader looks at the chart and thinks, "I should have seen that." In real time, the same move was one of several plausible outcomes. The illusion of obviousness in retrospect feeds overconfidence going forward. The cure is humility about what you actually saw before the move, not after it.

Anchors and arbitrary numbers

Traders anchor on entry prices, on round numbers, on prior highs and lows, on whatever number happens to be visible on the screen. "Holding until it gets back to even" is the textbook example. The market has no idea what your entry price was and no obligation to return to it. Decisions made relative to arbitrary anchors instead of relative to expected value are a steady source of error.

Sunk costs

Hours studied, courses bought, money already lost — they are sunk. They cannot affect the next trade. Yet many traders escalate precisely because of those sunk investments: "I cannot quit now, I have put in two years." The mature accounting treats sunk cost as paid. The only relevant question is the forward expected value of the next decision, taken as if no past decision had committed you to anything.

The slot-machine mind

Brain-imaging studies of traders show that the anticipation of an uncertain reward activates the same circuits as gambling and drug use. The schedule of trading — most attempts produce nothing, occasional ones produce big wins, the timing is unpredictable — is the most addictive schedule known to behavioral psychology. It is not a coincidence that mobile trading apps now have confetti animations. The design is borrowed from the casino.

Stress and tired decisions

Cognitive performance under sleep deprivation, financial stress, or extended screen time degrades measurably. Pilots have hard rest rules for this reason. Day traders, working alone, often trade in cognitive states that would ground a commercial pilot. Decisions made in those states tend to be impulsive, large, and bad.

Process beats willpower

The most reliable defense against all of this is structure. Rules that are written down, sized in advance, and executed mechanically reduce the moment-by-moment role of emotion. Lower account size, fewer screens, lower leverage, longer holding periods, and complete absence of trading apps from the phone — all are structural changes that work even when the trader's willpower fails. The trader who relies on willpower alone is competing against a system designed to exhaust it.

How professional traders manage their minds

Professional traders, the ones who survive in the business for decades, generally do not rely on willpower. They rely on routines. They keep regular sleep hours. They exercise. They eat real meals at consistent times. They write down each trade, including the reason for taking it and the conditions under which they would close it. They review their decisions weekly with peers who have no stake in being polite.

The point of these routines is not virtue. It is to take as much of the decision-making as possible out of the moment of pressure. Decisions made while calm are usually better than decisions made while losing. Routines that protect the calm version of the trader from the panicked one are some of the most valuable things a serious participant can build.

The journal as the cheapest tool

A trading journal is one of the cheapest, most disliked, and most useful tools available. It costs nothing to keep. It works because it forces the trader to write down their actual reason for taking a trade, before the outcome is known, and then to compare the reason to the outcome later. Most retail traders do not keep journals because the comparison is uncomfortable. The discomfort is exactly why the journal helps. It surfaces the difference between what the trader thinks they are doing and what they are actually doing.

The format does not matter. A spreadsheet works. A notebook works. The columns that matter are: date, instrument, entry price, exit price, position size, dollar result, and one sentence each for the reason and the lesson. After fifty trades, patterns appear. After two hundred, the trader has more honest information about themselves than any course can provide.

The case for trading less

Almost every emotional problem described in this chapter gets smaller when the trader trades less often. Fewer trades mean fewer decisions made under pressure, fewer outcomes that need to be processed, fewer round-trip costs, and more time between sessions for the body and the mind to recover. There is no badge for trading frequently. The market does not know how busy you have been.

If you are trading and reading this, an experiment worth running is to cut your number of trades in half for the next month. Not your position size, not your strategy — just your frequency. Most retail traders find that their results improve, their stress levels drop, and their relationships at home get easier. The change costs nothing and risks nothing. It is one of the few free improvements available.

The pre-trade checklist

A short pre-trade checklist, written down before the trade is taken, removes much of the emotional reasoning that sneaks into live decisions. The questions on the list do not have to be sophisticated. They can be as simple as: What is the thesis? What price would prove me wrong? What is the position size? Have I checked that this size respects my daily and weekly loss limits? Am I emotionally calm right now, or am I trading to feel something? If a trade fails the checklist, it does not happen.

Most retail traders skip this step because it slows them down. The slowing down is the point. Almost every trade taken without a written-down thesis is a trade taken under emotional logic. The journal entry that follows is rarely honest about that. The checklist forces the trader to be honest before the trade rather than after.

How losses feel different than the spreadsheet shows

On a spreadsheet, a thousand-dollar loss is a number. In real life, the same loss feels different depending on what else is happening. After a string of wins, it feels like an annoying interruption. After a string of losses, it feels like the beginning of the end. With money the trader can comfortably afford to lose, it feels like the cost of doing business. With money that was meant for rent, it feels like panic.

The trader's strategy was probably designed assuming the spreadsheet view. The trader's actual decisions are made in the felt view. The gap between the two is where most trading mistakes live. The protections are structural — keep position sizes small enough that losses feel like the spreadsheet view, not the panic view, and keep capital walled off from money meant for anything else, so that no single trade can intersect with rent.

Why the brain treats losses as physical threats

The human brain, evolved over millions of years, treats financial losses as if they were physical threats. The amygdala — the brain region that handles fear responses — activates in response to a position moving against you, much as it would if a predator appeared at the edge of camp. The body produces stress hormones. Heart rate rises. Attention narrows. The decisions made in this state are biased toward immediate action: fight, flee, or freeze.

None of these responses are well-suited to patient analysis of a market position. The trader who experiences a sharp adverse move and immediately closes the position is following the brain's threat response, not a financial calculation. Sometimes closing was the right answer. Often it was not. The honest practice is to recognize when the brain is in threat mode and refuse to make decisions in that state. Walk away. Eat. Sleep. Return when calm. The market will be there. The position can wait. Decisions made under threat physiology are reliably worse than decisions made when the body is back to baseline.

How professionals build emotional discipline

Professional traders who survive in the business for decades almost always develop similar emotional habits. They keep regular sleep schedules. They exercise. They have hobbies that have nothing to do with markets. They limit their screen time. They take real vacations. They talk regularly to other people who are not in the business, about things that are not markets.

The point of these habits is not virtue. It is to keep the trader's nervous system from being entirely shaped by markets. A trader whose only experience is screens and price action loses the perspective that comes from a fuller life. Their emotional reactions narrow. Their decisions get tighter and worse. The professional who survives is the one whose life is wide enough that any single trading day, good or bad, is a small part of it. The retail trader whose life has narrowed to the screen is operating without that protection, and the narrowing is one of the most reliable signs that the activity has become a problem.

Sleep is the cheapest discipline

Among the protective behaviors available to a trader, regular sleep is the cheapest and one of the most effective. A trader sleeping seven or eight hours a night makes measurably better decisions than the same trader sleeping five or six. The difference is not subtle. It shows up in reaction time, in working memory, in emotional regulation, in willingness to follow rules under pressure.

Most retail traders treat sleep as flexible — something to compromise when markets demand attention. The result is that decisions are made by an impaired version of themselves, often during the most stressful sessions, when impaired decisions are most expensive. The protective discipline is to treat sleep as non-negotiable. Markets will continue without you. Positions can be closed before bedtime. The trader who insists on sleeping enough is making a decision that improves every other decision they will make tomorrow. Few investments produce that compounding return.

> *The market is not testing your intelligence. It is testing your nervous system, and the nervous system loses by default unless protected by structure.*

Chapter 11

Leverage and Borrowed Money

Leverage is the single most consequential feature of retail trading. Used carefully, it can adjust the risk profile of a portfolio. Used the way most retail traders use it, it converts a difficult activity with negative expected value into a fast-acting wealth destroyer. Investor.gov, the U.S. Securities and Exchange Commission's public investor education site, warns explicitly that leveraged strategies amplify losses and require active management most investors are not equipped to provide.

What leverage actually means

If you control one hundred thousand dollars of exposure with ten thousand dollars of your own money, you are levered ten to one. A one percent move in the underlying produces a ten percent change in your equity. A ten percent move against you wipes you out. The arithmetic runs the same way in both directions. The asymmetry that matters is on the downside: a fifty percent loss requires a one hundred percent gain to recover, and on a leveraged account the loss arrives faster than the recovery.

How much leverage by venue

- U.S. equities under standard margin rules: up to two to one overnight, four to one intraday for pattern day traders with at least twenty-five thousand dollars in equity.
- U.S. futures: very high effective leverage on day-trading margin. A single E-mini S&P contract represents hundreds of thousands of dollars of exposure on a margin of a few hundred dollars.
- Retail forex outside the U.S.: one hundred to one or higher is common. At those levels, a one percent move ends the

account.

- Crypto perpetual futures on offshore venues: up to one hundred to one on coins that routinely move five percent or more in a session.
- Long options: implicit high leverage in delta terms. Short-dated options near the money can deliver a ten-fold gain or a total loss on small underlying moves.

The risk of ruin

Risk of ruin is the chance that an account hits a defined critical drawdown — say, fifty percent — at any point during a sequence of trades. The qualitative truth is more important than the formula: as the size of each bet grows relative to your equity, the probability of ruin grows non-linearly. Two traders with the same edge but different bet sizes face wildly different long-run survival rates.

A short worked example. Suppose a strategy wins fifty-five percent of the time, with average wins equal to average losses, and the trader risks two percent of equity per trade. Long-run risk of ruin is small. Now raise the per-trade risk to ten percent of equity. Same edge. Risk of ruin rises into the tens of percent. Raise it again to twenty-five percent, and ruin becomes the most likely outcome regardless of the edge. Many small accounts run by retail traders are operating in the third regime without realizing it.

Stops do not save you from gaps

A stop-loss order does not guarantee that you exit at the stop price. It triggers a market order at the stop, and in fast markets — gaps, halts, fast news — the actual fill can be far from the trigger. Documented examples include flash crashes where stops set at "safe" levels filled at prices fifty percent below the trigger. Stops reduce expected loss size. They do not cap it.

Margin spirals

The most painful leverage outcomes are not single losses; they are spirals. The position moves against you. The broker raises maintenance margin, often during the very stress that caused the loss. You add capital from a side account, hoping for recovery. You do not get it. You add more. The capital you added is also gone. The spiral is so common in regulator consumer-protection materials that it has its own paragraph in the SEC's leveraged-investing warnings.

Borrowed money makes everything worse

Trading on margin is leverage from the broker. Trading with money borrowed from somewhere else — credit cards, home equity, personal loans, family — adds household debt to account losses. The same dollar of loss now compounds into late fees, missed payments, damaged credit, and the kind of harm that takes years to repair. Regulators consistently identify this as one of the main paths from "trading hobby" to financial catastrophe.

When leverage is appropriate

There is a respectable use of leverage. A long-term investor with stable income may modestly leverage a diversified portfolio to harvest market returns more efficiently. Done at low ratios, with cheap financing, on broad and diversified positions, by an investor who can survive long drawdowns, this is defensible. It looks nothing like a retail trader at twenty to one on a single stock or one hundred to one on a currency pair. The case for leverage exists. The retail use of it usually does not.

What leverage feels like in real numbers

Imagine you have ten thousand dollars in a trading account. With no leverage, the worst day you can have is a day where every position goes to zero and you lose ten thousand dollars. With ten-to-one leverage, you can control one hundred thousand dollars of exposure. A ten percent move against you, in a single day, takes the entire account. Many days, in many markets, contain ten percent moves.

With twenty-to-one leverage — common in retail futures and options — a five percent move ends the account. With one hundred-to-one leverage, common in offshore retail forex, a one percent move ends it. These are not unusual moves. They happen all the time. The arithmetic of high leverage is that the trader is no longer asking whether the position will work eventually. They are asking whether it will work before it temporarily moves an ordinary amount in the wrong direction. That is a much harder question.

The recovery problem

Losses and gains are not symmetric. If you lose ten percent of your account, you need an eleven percent gain on what is left to break even. Lose twenty percent, and you need a twenty-five percent gain. Lose fifty, and you need a hundred. Lose seventy-five, and you need three hundred. Lose ninety, and you need nine hundred percent — a tenfold gain — to recover.

This is why drawdowns are so dangerous, and why leverage makes them more dangerous. A leveraged trader who suffers a series of losing days can find themselves in a position from which mathematical recovery is unrealistic. The remaining account is too small, and the gains required to rebuild are too large. They can keep trading, hoping for a hot streak, but the hot streak required is no longer plausible. This is the path that ends accounts.

When the broker decides for you

Most leveraged accounts have what is called a maintenance margin requirement. If your equity falls below a defined level, the broker can sell your positions without your consent to bring the account back into compliance. This is called a margin call. It usually happens at the worst possible moment — when the market is moving against you fastest, when liquidity is thin, when prices are at their most disadvantageous.

Margin calls are not a hypothetical risk. Every active leveraged trader will eventually face one if they continue long enough. The defense is to use less leverage than the broker allows, keep extra cash in the account as a buffer, and avoid concentrating the entire account in one or two highly correlated positions. Even with these defenses, severe market events can force liquidations that no plan can fully prevent. The only complete defense is to avoid leverage altogether, which is what most patient long-term investors do.

Borrowed money outside the brokerage

Some of the worst trading outcomes do not come from broker leverage. They come from money borrowed from outside sources to fund trading: credit cards, personal loans, home equity lines, money borrowed from family. The trader convinces themselves that the next trade will recover everything. The next trade does not. The borrowed money is now lost, and the obligation to repay it remains.

Regulators consistently identify outside borrowing as one of the leading causes of severe household financial harm related to trading. The rule is simple and worth following without exception: never trade with money you do not own outright. If you cannot afford to lose it from your own savings, you cannot afford to risk it. No exception is worth the financial unraveling that follows when borrowed-money trading goes wrong.

Why even the smart get hurt by leverage

The history of finance is full of intelligent people who lost large sums to leverage. Long-Term Capital Management, the famous hedge fund founded by elite practitioners including Nobel laureates, used substantial leverage on strategies that had positive expected value under normal conditions. In 1998, a series of correlated moves the model considered very unlikely actually happened, and the leverage that magnified the strategy's modest edge magnified the unusual losses into existential ones. The fund had to be rescued by a consortium of banks.

The lesson is not that leverage is always wrong. The lesson is that leverage applied to a strategy with positive expected value converts the question from "will this work eventually" to "will this work before something unusual but possible happens." That is a much harder question. A retail trader using high leverage is asking the same hard question on smaller scale, with worse information, and without the bank consortium standing by to rescue them when the answer is no.

Stop-losses are not safety nets

A stop-loss is a market order that becomes active when the price reaches a chosen level. In normal market conditions, it executes at or near that level, which is what most traders expect. In abnormal conditions — gaps overnight, halts during news, fast moves in thin markets — the actual execution can be far worse than the trigger price. Documented examples include flash crashes where stops set at "safe" levels filled at prices fifty percent below those levels before liquidity returned a few minutes later.

The implication is that stops reduce expected loss size but do not cap it. A trader sizing positions on the assumption that the stop will always work as intended is building a system that occasionally fails catastrophically. The honest sizing assumes that some percentage of stops will execute much worse than planned, and that the worst-case scenarios — gap risk on overnight positions, halts on individual stocks — are real and recurring rather than theoretical.

When the broker becomes the seller

In severe market stress, brokers liquidate customer positions to protect themselves. The trader's positions are not sold thoughtfully or at favorable prices; they are sold at whatever prices the market offers in the moment. During flash events — a major economic surprise, a coordinated selloff, a cryptocurrency exchange collapse — these forced liquidations have produced fills dramatically worse than the trader expected, sometimes wiping accounts that would have survived if the broker had waited even an hour.

This is not the broker behaving unfairly. It is the broker following the rules of margin trading, which exist precisely because customers cannot be relied on to close positions in time. The defense is to use less leverage than the broker allows, hold extra equity in the account as a buffer, and accept that any market position large enough to require margin is also large enough to be liquidated by the broker at the worst possible moment. The patient investor with no margin avoids this entire category of risk by structural choice.

Why patient investors use little or no leverage

Across the long history of patient investing, the most successful practitioners have generally used little or no leverage on their own portfolios. They could afford it. Banks would have lent to them. They chose not to, because they understood that leverage converts a high-probability long-term gain into a much harder question about whether the position survives the path.

The point is not that leverage is always wrong. The point is that the patient investor's edge — time, compounding, the productive growth of underlying businesses — does not require leverage. It requires only patience and consistent contribution. Adding leverage to that strategy adds risk without much corresponding benefit. The investor who chooses no leverage gives up some upside in good years in exchange for the certainty of surviving bad ones, and surviving bad ones is the precondition for everything else.

What 'just a little leverage' actually adds

Some traders argue that a small amount of leverage — say, two to one or three to one — is reasonable, because the math is not extreme. The argument has some merit at modest leverage levels, applied to broadly diversified positions, by investors who can survive long drawdowns. It also misses an important asymmetry: even small leverage materially increases the chance of being forced out of a position at the worst moment.

An unlevered investor in a diversified portfolio, holding through a thirty percent drawdown, eventually sees the recovery and benefits from it. The same investor at two to one leverage, holding through the same drawdown, may have already been liquidated by the broker, locking in a sixty percent loss with no chance of riding the recovery. The leverage did not change the underlying gain or loss of the investment. It changed whether the investor was still in the position when the recovery came. The unlevered investor was. The levered one often is not.

> *If you do not know your risk of ruin, your risk of ruin is high.*

Chapter 12

Market and Charts Manipulation

Markets are not perfectly fair. Some forms of manipulation are obvious frauds and well-prosecuted. Others are legal but expensive to the people on the wrong end. A retail trader who reads a price chart without understanding what is happening behind it is reading a partly forged document.

Pump and dump

The simplest kind. A small group buys a thinly traded stock or token cheaply, then promotes it heavily — paid newsletters, social media campaigns, coordinated chat-room hype. Retail buyers pile in. The early group sells into the rising price. The buying eventually stops, the price collapses, and the late arrivals hold the loss. The pattern is documented across small-cap stocks, crypto tokens, and unregistered foreign-exchange schemes. The chart looks like a moonshot followed by a cliff.

Spoofing and layering

Spoofing means placing large orders without intending to execute them, then canceling them after the price has moved in response. Layering is similar — stacking fake orders at multiple levels to create the impression of one-sided pressure. Both are illegal and have produced successful prosecutions, including very large fines. They also persist at smaller scales because regulators cannot watch every venue at every moment. A retail trader reading the order book without knowing about these tactics is sometimes reading orders that were never going to fill.

Painting the tape

"Painting the tape" is coordinated trading among related parties to make a stock look more active than it really is. Volume spikes that look like institutional interest can sometimes be circular — the same parties buying from each other to create a chart that pulls in outside buyers. This is more common in low-volume stocks and in some corners of the crypto market.

Stop hunting

Stop-loss clusters above round numbers and obvious levels are not secret. Algorithmic traders know exactly where they sit. When the broader tape allows it, those clusters become magnets: price gets pulled toward them, the stops trigger a cascade, and the move quickly reverses. The retail trader who placed the textbook stop just above the textbook level was the prey. The lesson is not to give up on stops but to place them with awareness of where the obvious clusters are.

Front running and high-frequency activity

Most high-frequency trading is legal market-making — providing liquidity in exchange for the spread. Some of it shades into behavior that looks more like front-running retail order flow, by reacting to detected retail activity faster than the retail trader can re-quote. The structural feature here is that retail flow is statistically less informed, on average, than institutional flow, and wholesale firms pay brokers for access to it precisely because the asymmetry is profitable.

Broker incentives

Even legitimate, regulated brokers have incentives the user should understand. Payment for order flow grows with order count. Margin lending grows with leverage. Securities lending grows with the broker's ability to lend customer holdings to short sellers. Cash sweeps earn the broker the spread between the rate paid to you and the rate the broker earns. None of this is illegal, but none of it aligns cleanly with the customer's long-term wealth. The investor who trades less costs the broker something on every line. The investor who trades constantly is paying through every channel.

Charts that lie by selection

Beyond active manipulation, charts mislead through selection. The success stories of any strategy are visible. The failures are not. Screenshots of profitable trades populate every social-media feed. Screenshots of margin calls do not. The trader who learns from public material is learning from a sample biased toward the survivors. Adjusting for that bias is hard and rarely done.

What this chapter is not saying

It is not saying every market move is manipulated. The vast majority of price action reflects genuine, decentralized buying and selling. It is saying that pure technical reading of charts assumes a clean, honest signal that is not always there. A trader who knows that some part of what they see is engineered — by manipulators on the worst days, by predictable structural flows on the rest — will make better decisions than a trader who treats the chart as truth.

How to spot a pump in progress

Coordinated pumps follow recognizable patterns. The chart of the pumped asset moves up sharply on heavy volume, often for no clear fundamental reason. Social-media accounts you have never heard of suddenly post enthusiastic content about it. Online forums fill with anonymous accounts predicting it will go much higher. Press releases appear, sometimes from dubious sources. The promotion gets louder as the price rises.

If you find yourself suddenly aware of an asset because of a wave of online attention, you are probably looking at a pump in progress. The early participants are the ones who profit. The late participants are the ones who fund those profits. The honest response, almost always, is to stay out. The asymmetric outcome — small chance of joining late and getting out in time, large chance of being the exit liquidity — is not worth the trade.

Why "smart money" leaves footprints you cannot follow

Some retail traders try to follow institutional flow by watching unusual options activity, large block trades, or insider filings. The intuition is reasonable: the people who know more should leave traces of their decisions. The problem is that the traces are usually visible only after the move has already happened, and the traces themselves are sometimes deliberately misleading.

Large institutions break up their orders to avoid signaling intent. They use dark pools, where trades print without showing up on the visible tape until later. They use derivatives that hide the true position. By the time a retail trader sees "unusual activity," the institution has often finished its move. The retail trader following the trace arrives in time to be the exit, not the entry.

What the SEC and FINRA actually do

The U.S. Securities and Exchange Commission and FINRA pursue a steady stream of manipulation cases. Spoofing prosecutions have produced hundreds of millions of dollars in settlements. Insider trading enforcement has put high-profile defendants in prison. Market-wide rules — circuit breakers that pause trading after extreme moves, position limits in commodity futures, registration requirements for brokers — exist because regulators have seen what happens when they do not.

The system is not perfect. Manipulation that involves smaller markets and faster venues is harder to police, and many bad actors operate from jurisdictions where U.S. regulators have no reach. But the existence of regulation matters for retail traders. Trading at registered, regulated venues with audited financials is the difference between participating in a market with rules and participating in a market without them. Where the rules apply, the worst behavior is at least constrained. Where the rules do not apply, anything goes.

Where retail flow goes, exactly

When a retail trader places an order through a commission-free app in the U.S., the order does not usually go directly to a stock exchange. It goes first to a wholesale market maker — a firm that pays the broker for the right to fill the order. The wholesaler matches the order against their own inventory, often at a price slightly better than the public quote, and pockets the spread. The arrangement is legal, disclosed in fine print, and profitable for both the broker and the wholesaler.

From the retail trader's perspective, the fill is often slightly better than the displayed quote, which feels like a small win. From the wholesaler's perspective, the average retail order is statistically less informed than the average institutional order, which means filling retail flow is profitable on average. The structure is not a scam. It is a system that earns its participants money by routing orders to the participants best equipped to capture spread from them. The retail trader gets a fair fill on most days. They also pay, in a less visible way, for the convenience of the system.

How to protect yourself from manipulation

Most manipulation that affects retail traders happens in small, illiquid securities. The defenses are mostly about avoiding the most-manipulated venues. Trade liquid, well-followed names rather than thin penny stocks. Stay out of small-cap names that suddenly appear in your feed with no obvious news. Skip the assets being promoted heavily on social media by accounts you do not know. Refuse to participate in chat-room "plays" that depend on coordinated buying.

None of this is a guarantee. Manipulation occasionally reaches larger names. But the probability of being on the wrong end of a coordinated scheme is dramatically lower in well-established markets than in the corners where promoters operate. Choosing where you participate is one of the most consequential ways to reduce manipulation risk, and it costs nothing.

How to spot a manipulated chart

Some charts have a recognizable shape that suggests manipulation rather than genuine market interest. A small-cap stock that was trading flat for months, then suddenly rises on heavy volume to many multiples of its previous price, often with no news event that would justify the move, is a classic pattern. A token that was priced near zero, then climbs ten or twenty times in a week, accompanied by waves of social-media promotion, is the same shape in a different market.

These shapes do not appear in clean, well-functioning markets. They appear in venues where promoters can move price without much resistance from other participants. Recognizing the shape is itself a defense. The honest response, almost always, is to stay out. The promoters need late buyers to provide their exit. The reader who declines to be that late buyer has avoided one of the most reliable categories of retail loss.

What clean markets look like

Most well-known stocks, in regulated jurisdictions, trade in markets that are essentially clean. Manipulation, where it exists, tends to concentrate in smaller, less-followed names, in venues with thinner regulation, and in moments of unusual market stress. A reader who chooses to trade only large, liquid, well-followed instruments in regulated markets is operating in conditions where the worst forms of manipulation are unlikely to affect them directly.

This is not a guarantee. Even large markets have bad days, and even regulated venues have occasional failures. But the difference in risk between large-cap U.S. stocks and small-cap penny stocks is enormous. The same is true for major cryptocurrencies versus newly launched tokens. Choosing where to participate is one of the cheapest defenses against manipulation, and most readers underweight it.

Why social-media stock tips usually lose

A specific kind of manipulation has grown alongside social media. An anonymous account or a viral video promotes a small, thinly traded stock. Retail buyers pile in. The price rises sharply on the retail volume. The promoters, who bought before the promotion started, sell into the buying. The price collapses as the promotional wave subsides. Most retail buyers, who arrived after the promotion peaked, sit on losses they cannot recover.

The pattern is so common that careful retail traders treat any sudden viral attention to a small stock as a warning sign rather than as a buy signal. The promoters are not stupid. They picked the stock for its thinness, which makes it easy to push the price. They picked the timing for the moment they would benefit most. The retail buyer who joined late is, by design, the exit liquidity. Recognizing the pattern is one of the cheapest defenses available.

Chapter 13

Day Trading Hidden Fees

"Free" trading is one of the most successful pieces of financial marketing of the last two decades. The headline cost of a retail stock trade has fallen to zero. The actual cost of a round trip — every component the trader pays, directly and indirectly — has fallen far less than the headline suggests. For active day traders, the total can dwarf any plausible profit.

The full list of costs

- Spread: the difference between bid and ask, paid every round trip. On a typical large stock, about one basis point. On smaller names, five to twenty-five basis points. On small crypto tokens, much more.
- Commission: zero on most U.S. retail apps for stocks, but still present on options (per contract), futures (per contract), and many international markets.
- Slippage: the gap between the price you expected and the price you got. Small in calm markets and large in fast ones, especially for market orders.
- Financing: margin interest on long leverage, which can run from eight to thirteen percent annually at retail brokers, and rebate fees on short positions.
- Data and platform fees: real-time market data subscriptions, charting platforms, news feeds, premium memberships. A serious day-trading setup can cost several hundred dollars a month.
- Taxes: short-term gains in the U.S. are taxed at the trader's ordinary income rate, often more than double the long-term capital gains rate.
- Time: hours at the screen that could have produced wages, learning, rest, or relationships. Most traders never put a number on this. They should.

A worked example

A trader takes ten round trips per session, two hundred sessions per year, on liquid U.S. stocks. Round-trip cost: about one basis point of spread plus a few of slippage, call it eight basis points total. With ten thousand dollars of equity rotated five times per day, the daily notional traded is fifty thousand dollars, and the daily cost is forty dollars. Over two hundred trading days, eight thousand dollars — eighty percent of the starting account — paid in costs alone. The strategy must produce eighty percent gross return on equity merely to break even before tax. The trader who clears that and pays short-term tax on the rest has a punishing path to net wealth.

Tax friction is real

Short-term capital gains are taxed at the trader's marginal ordinary income rate, which can exceed thirty-five percent at the federal level alone, plus state. Long-term gains on positions held over a year are taxed at preferential rates. On the same gross return, long-term holding versus short-term flipping can produce twenty-five percent or more difference in net result over time. Wash-sale rules add another layer of complexity that catches inexperienced traders by surprise when the tax forms arrive.

What "free" actually costs

Brokers that advertise zero commissions earn substantial revenue from payment for order flow, margin lending, securities lending, options order flow, and cash-sweep spreads. None of those are inherently wrong. All of them are real costs to the client, just located somewhere other than the headline commission line. A serious trader compares total transaction costs across brokers, not advertised commissions, and pays attention to which broker's incentives are most aligned with their actual goals.

The investor's cost stack, by contrast

A long-term investor in a low-cost broad-market index fund pays an expense ratio of three to ten basis points per year. They generate almost no taxable events. They incur essentially zero spread cost on the small number of buys executed. Annual cost on a hundred-thousand-dollar account: thirty to a hundred dollars. Annual cost for an active day trader of the same size: thousands. Compounded across decades, that gap is one of the most underrated drivers of differences in household wealth.

Adding it all up over a year

Take a hypothetical trader. They have an account of fifteen thousand dollars. They trade six round trips per session, two hundred sessions per year. The average position is five thousand dollars. The bid-ask spread averages three basis points (0.03 percent). Slippage averages four basis points. Commissions on options or futures (if they trade those) are fifty cents per contract. They subscribe to a charting platform at thirty dollars a month and a news service at fifty dollars a month.

The annual spread cost: 6 trades × 200 days × $5,000 × 0.0003 × 2 (round trip) = $1,800. Slippage: another $2,400. Subscriptions: $960. Even with no commissions, the trader has paid more than five thousand dollars in annual costs — over a third of the starting account — before any taxes are paid. To break even, the strategy must produce at least a thirty-three percent return on equity. To produce a ten percent net profit, the strategy must produce more than forty-three percent. Few retail strategies do.

The opportunity cost of time

Above all the visible costs sits the invisible one: the trader's time. A day trader who spends thirty hours a week on the activity, fifty weeks a year, invests fifteen hundred hours. At any reasonable hourly rate the trader could have earned doing other work, that is a substantial dollar value. A trader earning the equivalent of fifty dollars an hour at their day job is putting seventy-five thousand dollars of opportunity cost into a hobby that, on average, loses money.

Few retail traders include this in the calculation. They should. The honest accounting of "how much did trading cost me last year" includes not only the realized losses and the explicit fees but also the hours that could have produced wages, learning, exercise, sleep, and time with family. Most active retail trading, when fully accounted, is one of the most expensive hobbies a person can have.

Why long-term investing wins on costs alone

A long-term investor in a low-cost index fund pays an annual fee of three to ten basis points. On a fifteen-thousand-dollar account, that is between four-fifty cents and fifteen dollars per year. There is no spread to pay on most days, because there is no trading on most days. There is no slippage worth mentioning. There is no platform subscription required. There is no opportunity cost in time, because the strategy requires almost no time.

Compare that to the day trader's five thousand dollars in costs. Across thirty years, with the same gross investment performance, the cost difference alone produces dramatically different end balances. This is one of the most underrated reasons why patient investors usually outperform active retail traders even when both have access to the same markets, the same information, and the same starting capital. The patient ones simply pay less to participate.

The two minutes per trade you do not see

When a retail trader places a market order, the journey of that order takes a couple of seconds in the trader's experience. Behind the scenes, the order may pass through several systems: the broker's risk checks, a wholesale market maker's pricing engine, an exchange or alternative trading system, the clearing process. Each step takes milliseconds and adds tiny costs. Aggregated across millions of orders, those tiny costs are how the financial-services industry earns billions of dollars per year from retail trading.

None of this is illegal or hidden in any deep sense. The disclosures exist in every brokerage agreement. They are also several pages long, written in legal language, and never read by most users. The practical consequence is that the trader who clicks Buy is participating in a system whose total costs are higher than the displayed commission of zero suggests. Knowing this does not change much; the trader cannot opt out of the system. But it does change how confidently the trader can claim that costs are trivial.

How short-term taxes change the math

U.S. tax code distinguishes between short-term capital gains (held one year or less) and long-term capital gains (held more than one year). Short-term gains are taxed at ordinary income rates, which can exceed thirty-five percent at the federal level alone, plus state. Long-term gains are taxed at preferential rates of zero, fifteen, or twenty percent depending on income. The same gross profit from holding a stock for thirteen months versus eleven months can differ by a substantial amount in net result.

Day traders, by definition, never qualify for long-term rates on their trading profits. This is a permanent tax disadvantage of the activity that is rarely included in retail performance comparisons. A trader earning twenty percent gross on their account, paying short-term tax, ends up with materially less than a long-term investor earning the same twenty percent and paying long-term rates. The boring path keeps more of the same gross return.

What a sustainable trading frequency would look like

If the math of trading costs is so unforgiving, what trading frequency could actually work for retail? The honest answer is much lower than most retail traders operate at. A trader who took two or three positions per month, held them for weeks, and aimed for moves of several percent each could potentially overcome costs if their decision-making was sound. The cost per round trip would be a much smaller fraction of the move targeted, and the reduced trading frequency would give the trader's mind and body time to recover between decisions.

Most retail traders do not operate this way because slow trading does not feel exciting. The very feature that makes it potentially profitable — the absence of constant action — makes it psychologically unappealing. The trader who can override that bias and trade infrequently is closer to the profile of a long-term investor than of a day trader, and the activity has converged toward something that might actually work. The trader who keeps clicking ten times a day, and who rationalizes the activity as "staying engaged," is paying for the engagement with their own returns.

How a small cost edge compounds

An investor in a fund charging one percent per year, compared to an investor in a fund charging 0.05 percent, gives up 0.95 percent annually. In a single year, that is small. Over thirty years, on a portfolio that grows at seven percent before fees, the difference is dramatic. The high-cost investor ends with substantially less than the low-cost investor, even though they made identical decisions about contributions and asset allocation.

The same arithmetic applies to trading costs, only more harshly. A retail trader giving up several percent per year to spread, slippage, and tax friction is operating with a permanent annual headwind that compounds against them. The patient investor with near-zero costs is operating with no such headwind. Across decades, the difference is one of the most underrated drivers of outcomes between households with similar incomes and similar starting savings. The household that minimized costs ended up significantly wealthier, simply because they paid less to participate in the same markets.

What costs look like in a single trade

Take a single hypothetical trade. The trader buys 100 shares of a stock at the asking price of $50.05. The bid is $50.00. The trader has already paid the spread on entry — five cents per share, fifty dollars total, just to be in the position. To exit at break-even on price, the stock must rise five cents. To make money, it must rise more than that. If the trader pays an additional cent of slippage on exit, the position must rise eleven cents just to cover round-trip costs.

On a fifty-dollar stock, eleven cents is roughly two-tenths of a percent. Markets move that much constantly, but they do not always move in the right direction. Across many trades, the small per-trade cost compounds into a substantial annual headwind. The trader who places a hundred trades like this per month is paying thousands of dollars per year in costs that the chart never displays. The chart shows price moves; the cost statement, if the trader bothered to read it, shows the real bottom line. Most retail traders never reconcile the two.

> *Costs are the only certainty in a market full of uncertainty. Minimize them and you have stacked the only deck you can stack.*

Chapter 14

Physical Health Risks

It is tempting to treat day trading as a clean cognitive activity, performed from a chair, with no obvious physical demands. That framing is wrong in ways that show up in clinic data and in the lived experience of long-time traders. The body pays a real price for sitting, for stress, for sleep disruption, and for the chemistry of constant uncertainty.

The sitting problem

Long sitting hours are an independent risk factor for heart disease, metabolic disorders, lower-back pain, and shortened life expectancy, even in people who exercise regularly. Active traders watching screens through the entire U.S. session, and often into European or Asian hours, easily exceed the daily sitting times that show up as harmful in research. Standing desks help only modestly. The behavior that actually protects you is regular movement breaks every twenty to thirty minutes — exactly what someone watching one-minute candles cannot bring themselves to take.

Stress chemistry

The body's response to short, sharp uncertainty is well documented: cortisol, adrenaline, blood pressure spikes. Repeated activation over years damages the cardiovascular system, the immune system, and metabolic regulation. A trader who experiences ten genuinely stressful position swings per day, two hundred days per year, is running a stress regime closer to that of an emergency-room physician — but without the social purpose, the team support, and the structured rest that help mitigate the load.

Sleep

Twenty-four-hour markets — forex, crypto, futures sessions — invite trading at hours that disrupt circadian rhythm. Even traders who only work U.S. cash hours often check positions late into the evening and grab the phone first thing in the morning. Fragmented sleep degrades immune function, metabolic health, and decision quality. A single night of partial sleep deprivation produces cognitive impairment comparable to mild alcohol intoxication. Trading on that level of impairment, with real money, is common and bad.

Eyes, neck, and posture

Multiple screens at close range produce digital eye strain, dryness, blurred vision, and headaches in a substantial share of long-duration users. Forward head posture, rounded shoulders, and weak posterior chain muscles develop over months and become structural over years. Physical therapists and chiropractors recognize the pattern as occupational. The fixes — desk height, monitor distance, lighting, regular standing — are well known and routinely skipped.

Eating, weight, and metabolism

Trading is conducive to disordered eating: quick snacks during active sessions, missed meals during stressful periods, late-night calorie loading after the close, and elevated alcohol use as a stress release. Combined with low daily activity, this pattern produces measurable weight gain, deteriorating cholesterol numbers, and rising fasting glucose over multi-year horizons. None of it is dramatic in any single year. All of it shows up in lab work over a decade.

Caffeine, nicotine, and stimulants

Caffeine consumption among active retail traders runs higher than population average. So does nicotine, particularly through vaping, which has become common in trading communities. A subset of traders escalate to prescription stimulants — Adderall and similar — sometimes diverted from legitimate prescriptions, sometimes purchased illicitly. The short-term focus boost is real. The medium-term cardiovascular cost, sleep degradation, and dependency liability are also real and far less discussed.

What helps

If you are going to spend long hours at a desk for any reason — investing, working, gaming — the protective behaviors are well established. A sit-stand desk. A monitor at arm's length and eye level. Frequent short movement breaks. Regular aerobic exercise. Ordinary, non-pharmacological sleep. Disciplined caffeine timing. None of these are luxuries. They are the basic maintenance work that lets a body keep showing up.

The deepest health protection a long-time trader can adopt, however, is the simplest: do less of it. Less time at the screen, smaller positions, longer holding periods. Each of those changes reduces exposure to the chemistry that does the damage.

What hours at a screen do over years

A trader who spends forty hours a week at a screen, fifty weeks a year, accumulates two thousand sitting hours per year. Across ten years, that is twenty thousand hours of sustained sitting under stress, with intermittent meals, irregular hydration, and limited movement. The body that began that experiment in good shape often ends it in noticeably worse shape: lower-back pain that becomes chronic, weight gain that resists episodic dieting, sleep that no longer recovers cleanly, lab values that drift in unhelpful directions.

None of this is dramatic in any single year. All of it is real over a decade. The damage is slow enough to be ignored and cumulative enough to be hard to undo. The trader who notices the pattern at thirty-five and changes course can recover. The trader who notices it at fifty has more work to do, and some of the changes are less reversible.

What actually helps

- A sit-stand desk used in both modes throughout the day, not just standing for an hour and sitting for the rest.
- A monitor at arm's length and at eye level — not below it, which is the default on most laptops.
- Movement breaks every twenty to thirty minutes, even brief ones. The point is not to exercise; it is to interrupt the sitting.
- Real meals at consistent times. Snacks at the desk are convenience food masquerading as fuel.
- Genuine sleep, in the dark, away from the phone. Trading apps off the bedroom is a small structural change with outsized benefits.
- A regular form of aerobic exercise outside the desk. Whatever you will actually do — walking, swimming, cycling, lifting — the answer is the one that gets done.

- Disciplined caffeine timing. Caffeine after noon is one of the most reliable causes of poor sleep that night, which is one of the most reliable causes of poor decisions the next day.

What does not help

Some popular fixes are popular because they are easy, not because they work. Standing all day instead of sitting all day produces a different set of problems. Energy drinks paper over fatigue without addressing it. Nicotine vaping is sold as a focus aid and produces the cardiovascular costs of nicotine use along with whatever else the device is delivering. Stimulant medications taken without prescription substitute one set of problems for another, often worse.

The healthier protocols are unfashionable because they are simple. Sleep, move, eat, hydrate, take breaks. The body does not need a hack. It needs the basic maintenance work that human bodies have always needed. Trading does not change that. It just makes it easier to skip.

Why cortisol matters

Cortisol is the body's main stress hormone. It is released in response to perceived threats and is helpful in short bursts — it sharpens attention, redirects blood flow, suppresses non-essential systems. Across days and weeks of repeated stress, however, chronic cortisol elevation produces a pattern of effects that medical research has documented carefully: elevated blood pressure, weight gain around the abdomen, suppressed immune function, disrupted sleep, and impaired memory consolidation.

A trader experiencing real stress every session is running their cortisol system harder than it was designed to be run. The body adapts in ways that feel like "normal" — the stressed state becomes the baseline — but the underlying systems are accumulating damage. The signs appear later: at first as small symptoms, then as lab values that drift in unhelpful directions, eventually as conditions that require medical treatment. The trader who could see the lab work twenty years in advance would treat their stress more seriously today.

Real recovery, not just rest

Recovery is more than the absence of trading. The body recovers from chronic stress through specific activities: aerobic exercise, deep sleep, social connection, meals at regular times, and time in environments that do not demand vigilance. The trader who closes the laptop and immediately opens the trading-news feed has not recovered. The trader who closes the laptop, takes a walk outside, eats a real meal with family, and goes to bed at a normal hour has.

The difference matters because recovery is when the damage from stress is repaired. Without it, the damage accumulates. With it, the trader can sustain a high-stress activity for years without the accumulating health costs that destroy long-time traders. The trader who chooses recovery routines deliberately is investing in the only asset that compounds faster than money — their own physical capacity to keep showing up.

The cost of long-term sleep debt

Sleep is not just rest. It is when the brain consolidates memory, the body repairs tissue, the immune system fights infections it has been holding off during the day, and the cardiovascular system gets a break from elevated demand. Chronic sleep restriction — six hours or less per night, sustained for weeks — produces measurable damage across all of these systems.

A trader who routinely goes to bed at one in the morning, wakes at six to check overnight markets, and tells themselves they are fine because they feel functional is running on a deficit the body is recording even when the mind cannot feel it. After a year or two, the deficit shows up as poor recovery from minor illnesses, weight gain that does not respond to dieting, irritability that strains relationships, and laboratory values that show the body is under stress. None of these effects are dramatic on any single day. All of them are real over time. Sleep is the single most under-protected element of the trader's health.

What aerobic exercise actually does for stressed traders

Aerobic exercise — walking briskly, jogging, cycling, swimming, anything that elevates the heart rate sustainably for thirty minutes or more — is one of the most reliable interventions for trading-related stress. The mechanism is direct and well documented: aerobic exercise reduces cortisol levels, improves sleep quality, releases endorphins, and produces a calmer baseline mood for hours afterward.

A trader who exercises four or five times a week is running a different chemical experiment in their body than one who does not. The exercising trader processes the day's stress through a system designed to handle it. The sedentary trader carries the stress unmetabolized, where it accumulates as the patterns described elsewhere in this chapter. Of all the protective behaviors available, regular aerobic exercise is one of the cheapest and most effective. It does not require a gym. It does not require equipment. It requires only consistency, which is the same trait that pays off in patient investing.

Why annual checkups matter for traders

An annual physical checkup, including basic blood work, is not optional for an active trader. The chronic stress of the activity produces measurable changes in the body that the trader cannot feel directly. Blood pressure, cholesterol, fasting glucose, inflammatory markers — these can drift in unhealthy directions for years before producing symptoms. The annual checkup catches the drift early, when the response can be lifestyle changes rather than medications or interventions.

Many traders skip checkups because they feel fine. Feeling fine is not the same as being fine. The point of monitoring is to catch problems before they reach the symptom stage. A trader who refuses to monitor is operating without one of the most basic forms of preventive care available, and is likely to discover the consequences only when the consequences have become harder to address.

What a one-week reset can show you

A reader who suspects trading has affected their physical health, but cannot tell how much, can run a simple test. For one week, change nothing about diet or exercise, but reduce screen time by half and sleep an extra hour each night. Pay attention to how the body feels by the end of the week. Most people who try this notice meaningful improvement: clearer thinking, calmer mood, better digestion, less low-grade pain. The improvement is not magical. It is the body responding to a small reduction in the stress and sleep deficit it had been carrying. The week-long test does not solve the underlying pattern, but it shows the trader what their body is capable of when not under chronic stress. That information alone often changes what the trader is willing to tolerate going forward.

The chair is not neutral. The screen is not neutral. The chemistry of uncertainty is not neutral. The body keeps the score.

Chapter 15

Mental Health Risks

The financial losses from failed day trading are visible. The mental health costs are less visible, often denied by the trader, and frequently larger in long-run impact. This chapter is not a clinical text. It is a candid summary of patterns that show up in research literature and in the testimony of people who have lived through them.

Anxiety and constant alertness

An active trading day is a string of uncertain decisions with money attached to each one. Sustained over months, the pattern produces meaningful anxiety symptoms in a substantial share of traders: tense vigilance during sessions, looping thoughts after hours, sleep disturbance, an exaggerated startle response. Generalized anxiety disorder presentations among active traders, in clinical reports, run substantially above general-population rates.

Depression after losses

A serious drawdown, especially one involving money the household cannot afford to lose, frequently triggers depressive episodes. Symptoms include loss of pleasure in normal activities, impaired concentration, withdrawal from family and friends, hopelessness, and in severe cases thoughts of self-harm. Financial loss and shame combine into a feedback loop in which the trader hides the loss to avoid the social cost of admitting it, which prolongs the isolation and deepens the depression.

Identity collapse

Many traders adopt trading as identity — "I am a trader, this is my path to freedom" — well before the evidence justifies the claim. When the activity fails, the loss is not just financial; it is an identity loss. Therapists who work with former traders describe a grief process not unlike the end of a career or the failure of a long-planned business. Recognizing trading as a habit rather than a destiny early in the engagement reduces the depth of the eventual reset.

Shame and secrecy

Shame is the operating fuel of most trading-related psychological harm. The trader cannot tell a spouse, parent, or friend about the size of the loss because, in the trader's own framing, the loss is evidence of personal failure. Hidden losses accumulate. Spouses learn months or years later. The discovery often dwarfs the original loss in relational damage. Honest, early communication is one of the most protective behaviors a trader can adopt; it is also the rarest.

Anger and blame

Loss is sometimes processed not as sadness but as anger. The trader blames brokers, market makers, regulators, manipulators, the news, the algorithm, the source of the trade idea. Some of these blames have partial truth. None of them produce useful change in the trader's behavior. Externalizing the source of error predicts longer engagement with losing strategies and slower recognition of the personal patterns that need to change.

When to seek help

If the descriptions above produce personal recognition, the most useful next step is talking to a licensed mental-health professional, ideally one familiar with addictive behaviors and financial stress. Cognitive-behavioral therapy has documented effectiveness for trading-related anxiety and compulsive trading patterns. National crisis lines exist in most jurisdictions for moments of acute distress, and the calls are free. None of this is a sign of weakness. It is a normal response to an environment optimized to produce these symptoms.

Structural protections

The most reliably protective measures against trading-related mental harm are structural rather than emotional. Limit account size to amounts whose total loss would not destabilize the household. Keep trading capital separate from emergency and retirement funds. Keep ordinary social and physical routines independent of session outcomes. Set real cooling-off periods after losses and enforce them with friction, not willpower.

The shame loop

Shame produces silence. Silence produces isolation. Isolation produces escalation, often with substances or further trading risk. Escalation produces larger losses. Larger losses produce deeper shame. The loop is self-sustaining once established and is most easily interrupted in its earliest phase, when the trader's losses are still moderate and the relationships in their life are still intact. Honest conversation with a partner, a friend, or a therapist before the loop deepens is the highest-leverage intervention available. The conversation feels harder than it is. The harm of not having it grows faster than most traders anticipate.

Recognizing the patterns in yourself

It is hard to see your own mental-health patterns clearly while you are inside them. A few signals are worth taking seriously. Sleep that no longer comes easily even when you are exhausted. Loss of pleasure in activities you used to enjoy. Irritability with family members about things that did not used to bother you. A constant low-level dread when you think about checking the account. Difficulty concentrating on anything that is not a chart. Persistent thoughts about money loss that intrude during meals, conversations, and time with children.

If two or more of these have been present for several weeks, the trader is in territory that warrants professional attention. This is not a sign of weakness. It is a normal response to an environment optimized to produce these symptoms. The earliest help is the cheapest help. The longer the symptoms continue, the harder they are to address.

What therapy actually does

Cognitive-behavioral therapy, the most common evidence-based approach for the patterns described in this chapter, is not mysterious. The therapist helps the patient identify thought patterns that produce specific feelings and behaviors, and works with them to test those patterns against reality. "I have to recover this loss today" is a thought. "This is the worst loss I have ever had" is a thought. Many of these thoughts, examined in a therapist's office, turn out to be inaccurate. Replacing them with more accurate thoughts changes how the patient feels and behaves.

Therapy does not require years of commitment. Many people see meaningful improvement in a few months of weekly sessions. The financial cost varies; in many places, employer health plans cover some or all of it. The cost of not getting help — financial, relational, and personal — is usually higher.

When the situation is urgent

If at any point you find yourself thinking about hurting yourself, the situation has become a medical emergency, not a financial one. National crisis lines exist in most countries and the calls are free. In the United States, dialing 988 reaches the Suicide and Crisis Lifeline. The call costs nothing, the conversation is confidential, and the person on the other end is trained for exactly this. Money problems are repairable. The other kind is not.

What a normal grief response looks like

When a trader takes a serious loss, particularly one that affects household plans, the response is often a grief response. The stages are well documented in clinical literature: shock and disbelief that the loss happened, anger at brokers or markets or themselves, bargaining with the future ("if I can just make it back"), depressive symptoms, and eventually acceptance and adaptation. The process is not pathological. It is what humans do when something significant has been lost.

Recognizing the response as grief, rather than as a sign of personal weakness, is itself protective. The trader who knows that the dark mood after a loss is a normal part of processing, not a personal flaw, is better positioned to wait it out without making impulsive decisions. The trader who interprets the dark mood as proof that something is wrong with them, by contrast, is more likely to escalate trading or substance use to escape the feeling. The first response leads through the loss; the second compounds it.

When professional help becomes essential

Some signs indicate that professional support has moved from optional to essential. Persistent symptoms (low mood, anxiety, sleep disturbance) for more than two weeks. Hidden behavior — accounts the partner does not know about, lies about exposure, growing secrecy. Substance use to manage trading-related stress that is escalating in frequency or quantity. Inability to step back from trading even when you have decided to. Any thoughts of self-harm or suicide.

The last item is a medical emergency. National crisis lines exist in most countries; in the United States, dialing 988 reaches a free, confidential service trained for exactly these moments. Money problems, even severe ones, can be repaired. The other kind of harm cannot. The cost of asking for help is zero. The cost of not asking, when help was needed, can be everything.

The role of meaning and purpose

Sustained mental health for adults depends, in part, on a sense of meaningful activity. People who feel that what they do matters — to their family, to their community, to a purpose larger than themselves — are more resilient to setbacks of all kinds. People whose primary daily activity is staring at price charts often find that this sense of meaning erodes over time, even if the trading is profitable.

The erosion is subtle. The trader notices that wins feel less satisfying than they used to. That losses feel more painful. That the days blur together. That conversations with non-traders feel small. The pattern is not a sign of personal failure. It is a sign that the activity is not feeding the parts of the human psyche that need feeding. Reintroducing meaning — through work that affects other people, through community involvement, through creative pursuits, through caring for others — is a mental-health intervention as real as any medication. Markets do not provide meaning. People and purpose do.

How to talk to someone about a friend

Some readers will recognize the patterns in this book in someone they care about — a spouse, a sibling, a friend, an adult child. The instinct is often to confront, to argue, to present evidence. The honest research on behavior change suggests that direct confrontation rarely works. The person being confronted defends, explains, and continues. The confrontation hardens the pattern rather than softening it.

What works better is a different kind of conversation. Express care, not criticism. Ask honest questions about how the person is feeling, not about what they are doing. Listen more than you talk. Mention that you have noticed changes — sleep, mood, social withdrawal — without attaching them to a specific behavior. Suggest professional resources without insisting. Then keep the relationship intact across many such conversations, over weeks and months. The behavior change, when it comes, usually comes from the person themselves, in response to a relationship that stayed steady. Confrontation accelerates the wrong direction. Patient presence, kept up over time, is what most people remember as having mattered when they finally changed.

What recovery looks like across years

Recovery from severe trading-related mental-health problems is not a quick process. The first weeks are often dominated by the immediate crisis: closing accounts, telling family, beginning treatment. The first months involve learning to live without the activity that organized so much of the previous routine. The first year often includes setbacks, relapses, and adjustments. The second year is usually calmer, with the trader rebuilding a life that no longer revolves around markets.

By the third or fourth year, most people who have committed to recovery describe themselves as in a different phase of life. The financial damage is being repaired through normal income and savings. The relationships have stabilized or improved. The body has recovered from much of the chronic stress. The trader looks back at the trading years as a difficult chapter that is now closed, rather than as the central feature of their life. This is the typical trajectory for people who actively seek help, follow through on it, and accept that the recovery is measured in years rather than months. The reader at the beginning of this trajectory should know that the long version of the recovery is real, achievable, and dramatically better than continuing on the path the recovery is leaving.

Why a single phone call can change a year

If you are reading this chapter and recognizing yourself in it, the most useful thing you can do today is also one of the simplest. Pick up the phone. Call your primary-care physician's office and ask for an appointment to discuss stress and mood. The appointment is confidential. The conversation is normal. The physician deals with these conversations every week. They will not be shocked. They will ask a few questions, perhaps suggest a screening tool, perhaps refer you to a counselor or a therapist.

The single phone call costs nothing. It does not commit you to anything. It opens a door that has been closed, and the opening alone often changes the year that follows. Most people who eventually recover from trading-related mental-health problems describe the moment of asking for help as the inflection point. Not the moment of recovery — that came later — but the moment when the trajectory shifted from worsening to improving. The call is the inflection. The reader who makes it has done something significant for their own future.

Trading harm is not weakness. It is the predictable product of a hostile environment plus inadequate structure.

Chapter 16

Personal Relationships

The relational cost of failed day trading shows up regularly in the testimony of recovered traders and in the practice notes of family therapists. It rarely shows up in trading literature, because it is private, painful, and hard to quantify. This chapter brings it into the open.

The information gap inside a household

Most trading happens behind a closed door. The spouse may know the activity exists; rarely does the spouse know the actual exposure, the real drawdown, or the source of the capital being deployed. The asymmetry is convenient in good months and devastating in bad ones. Discovery of a hidden trading loss — especially one funded by family savings, joint accounts, or borrowed money — is one of the most damaging events a marriage can absorb. It combines financial harm, broken trust, and the realization that the partner has been a stranger about the household's most consequential decision.

Time and attention

Active trading needs sustained attention during specific hours. For multi-asset traders, those hours are nearly continuous. The result is physical presence without psychological availability. A parent is at the dinner table but mentally on the closing print. A partner is on the weekend trip but consumed by the overnight crypto chart. A friend is at a celebration but checking a notification. Children, in particular, register this. They do not articulate it as "my parent is trading." They articulate it as "my parent is not here."

Mood transmission

Trading outcomes determine trading moods, and trading moods do not stay at the desk. A bad session carries into the evening as irritability, withdrawal, and short-tempered responses to ordinary household friction. The household learns to walk on eggshells around session outcomes. Children adapt by reducing their requests for attention. Spouses adapt by reducing emotional bids. Over years, the family becomes smaller in surface area, with fewer shared moments and less actual closeness.

Money decisions are partnership decisions

In any committed relationship, money decisions are shared. The trader who deploys household capital without joint consent — even when the deployment is technically legal in the jurisdiction's marital property regime — is making a unilateral decision with shared consequences. Reasonable partners can disagree about risk tolerance and savings rate. The disagreement is healthier when both have full information than when one is operating on incomplete data.

Recovery and repair

Relationships damaged by hidden trading can recover, but the path requires honesty earlier and more thoroughly than most traders are inclined to attempt. Disclosure of full exposure, joint review of the household balance sheet, structural commitments such as closed accounts and outside oversight, couples therapy, and time. The relationship that survives the disclosure has often metabolized something difficult into a stronger partnership. The relationship that survives only because the disclosure never happened is still carrying the unexploded ordnance.

The honest conversation

If you are trading and reading this, the most useful single action you can take this week is an honest conversation with your partner about exposure, drawdown, source of capital, time spent, and goals. The conversation is uncomfortable. The damage of not having it tends to be larger. A few specific questions cut through most of the noise:

- What is the maximum dollar loss the household can absorb without altering material plans?
- What share of household financial assets is currently exposed to trading?
- How much time per week is actually being spent on trading, including research and recovery from losses?
- What is the joint plan for the next six months — continue, reduce, or stop?
- Under what conditions, agreed in advance, does the activity stop?

Children notice

Children learn financial behavior largely from observation. A parent who appears stressed about money, who reacts visibly to market moves, who hides activity from the other parent, or who frames financial life as a contest of cleverness teaches a model of money the child carries forward. A parent who treats money plainly — budgets discussed openly, savings explained simply, big purchases planned together — teaches a different model.

The day-trading household, when its dynamics are dominated by session outcomes and concealed exposures, transmits the first model. The patient-investing household, when contributions are automated and reviewed calmly, transmits the second. Neither model is taught explicitly; both are absorbed across years of observation. The choice of which model to live in front of one's children is a financial-planning decision few investors articulate as such, and one of the most consequential.

How to start the conversation

If you are the trader and you have been hiding the size of your activity, the conversation with your partner is almost certainly going to be uncomfortable. There is no clever way around that. The most common path that works is also the simplest: a calm, private moment, an honest and complete account of where things actually stand, and a willingness to listen to your partner's response without rushing to defend yourself.

The disclosure should include the full account size, the realized losses to date, the source of any borrowed money, the time being spent, and the realistic outlook. The temptation will be to soften each number a little. The damage of softening is greater than the damage of the truth. A partner who eventually discovers that the disclosed numbers were optimistic feels twice betrayed — once by the original concealment, once by the incomplete confession.

Repair takes time

Relationships damaged by hidden financial activity can recover, but the path is longer than most people expect. Trust rebuilds through small, repeated demonstrations of new behavior, not through a single conversation. Joint review of the household balance sheet on a regular schedule, complete transparency about any continued trading activity, and willingness to involve a therapist or financial counselor when the conversations get stuck — all of these help. The relationship that emerges on the other side of an honest reckoning is often stronger than the one that existed before. The relationship that stays intact only because the truth never came out is still carrying the unexploded ordnance.

What financial transparency looks like in practice

A household with full financial transparency does a few specific things. Both partners know all the accounts and have access to the statements. Both partners review the household balance sheet regularly — once a quarter is plenty. Major financial decisions are discussed before they happen, not reported after. Investment activity, including any trading, is visible to both partners. Borrowing of any kind requires both signatures, in spirit if not legally.

This is not about distrust. It is about partnership. Two people who share a household share its financial life, and the version of the financial life that is honest is one where neither partner is surprised by what the other has been doing. Households that operate this way are not always richer than households that do not, but they tend to be calmer, more resilient to financial shocks, and more able to recover from mistakes.

When children are old enough to know

There is no perfect age at which to start talking with children about money, but the right age is earlier than most parents think. Young children can understand simple ideas — saving for a goal, the difference between things you need and things you want, the fact that money comes from work. Older children can understand more — the basics of investing, the concept of compounding, why the family makes the financial choices it does.

What children should generally not be exposed to is the parents' acute financial stress. They should know the family is being thoughtful with money. They should not be bearing the parents' anxiety about whether the trading account will recover. The line between age-appropriate honesty and adult anxiety is one parents have to think about deliberately. The children of the patient-investing household generally grow up calmer about money than the children of the chaotic-trading household, even when the dollar amounts at stake are similar.

Repair through small consistent acts

Relationships damaged by hidden financial activity rarely repair through grand gestures. They repair through small, consistent demonstrations of new behavior, sustained over months and years. The partner who was lied to about the trading account is not reassured by a single dramatic apology. They are reassured by hundreds of small interactions in which the trader behaves transparently, includes them in decisions, and follows through on commitments.

This is slower than the trader usually wants. The trader, having decided to be honest, is ready for the relationship to feel normal again immediately. The partner needs time to test whether the new behavior is real. Most relationships that recover from financial concealment do so on the partner's timeline, not the trader's. Accepting that timeline, without protest, is itself part of the repair.

Money meetings as a household practice

A household practice that quietly produces good financial outcomes: regular money meetings between partners. Once a month is plenty. The format is simple. Sit down for thirty minutes. Review the household's spending against the budget. Look at the investment accounts. Check that scheduled contributions are flowing. Note any large expenses coming up. Discuss any concerns either partner has. Adjust if needed. Adjourn.

These meetings are not exciting. They are also remarkably effective. Households that do them tend to be more aligned about money, less stressed about decisions, and more resilient to financial shocks. The practice creates a regular venue for things to be discussed, which means small concerns are addressed before they become large ones. The household that does not have such a venue often finds that money concerns build up in silence, surface during arguments about other things, and complicate decisions that should have been simple. The cost of the meeting is half an hour a month. The benefit is a household financial life that runs smoothly enough not to be a constant source of stress.

Why honesty produces better outcomes than hope

A trader who is hiding losses usually believes they will fix the situation before disclosure becomes necessary. The recovery trade, the hot streak, the breakthrough that will undo the damage — they tell themselves these are coming. Sometimes they are right. More often, they are wrong, and the eventual disclosure happens with much larger damage than the original hidden loss.

The honest practice is to disclose at the size of damage that exists today, not at the imagined size after the recovery that may never come. Today's damage is more recoverable than tomorrow's. Today's relationship can absorb a hard conversation more easily than next year's, after another twelve months of accumulating pressure. The trader who hopes their way into a worse disclosure is not protecting their family. They are protecting themselves from a hard conversation that is going to happen anyway, just later, when the conversation will be even harder.

What a partner notices first

Partners often notice patterns of trading-related stress before the trader does. The change in mood at certain times of day. The phone that is always nearby. The conversations that get cut short to check a chart. The vacation that was somehow not really a vacation because the markets did not stop. Partners watch these patterns develop and often hesitate to mention them, because the trader has framed the activity as something that should not be questioned.

A trader who values the relationship should make it easy for their partner to mention what they are seeing. Specifically inviting the conversation, listening without defending, and treating the partner's observations as data rather than as criticism — these are habits that protect the relationship and often improve the trading itself. The partner is closer to the trader's behavior than the trader is. Their observations are usually more accurate than the trader's self-assessment. Treating those observations as a gift, even when uncomfortable, is one of the cheapest ways to catch a developing problem early.

Chapter 17

Loneliness and Isolation

The retail-trader life, particularly for full-time participants, is one of the most isolating modern occupations. The work happens alone. The decisions happen alone. The wins are silent. The losses are silent. Long-time traders write about an emotional flatness that develops over years — neither the highs nor the lows feel as full as they once did, because they are being processed without witnesses.

Why isolation matters

Loneliness, in epidemiological research, is an independent risk factor for cognitive decline, heart disease, and earlier mortality. The size of the effect is comparable to well-known physical risks like smoking. The mechanisms are partly behavioral (less physical activity, worse sleep, more substance use) and partly direct, through the stress chemistry that chronic isolation activates. A trading life that systematically removes the trader from face-to-face human contact, most working hours, most days of the week, is not a neutral lifestyle choice.

Online communities are not replacements

Trading Discord servers, social-media feeds, and live streams provide a sense of community that is, in narrow respects, real. Other people are present. Conversation happens. But these relationships have a property that face-to-face friendships do not. They are mediated by the activity. Step away from the activity, and the community recedes. The friendships of someone who quit trading two years ago do not visit the hospital, attend the wedding, or help with the move. Friendships built across decades of shared life do.

The lifestyle freedom narrative

Trading is sold as freedom: work from anywhere, no boss, choose your own hours. The reality for most is the opposite. The trader works during whatever hours the chosen market trades, in whatever location has reliable internet, with a boss inside their own head running an unrelenting performance review. "Work from anywhere" tends to become "work from one specific room" because that room has the rig. "Choose your hours" tends to become "work all the hours" because the market does not stop and discipline is hard to enforce alone.

Conversation narrows

Heavy trading reshapes what the trader is willing to talk about. The market becomes the topic. Non-traders' subjects — work projects, parenting milestones, neighborhood politics — feel small in comparison. Over months, conversations with non-traders become effortful, and the trader gravitates toward other traders, where the shared idiom is fluent. The non-trader part of life shrinks. The narrowing is gradual and, by the time it is noticeable, deeply established.

Practical defenses

- Hold one weekly social ritual that has nothing to do with trading: a sport, a class, a meal with non-trading friends, a volunteer commitment.
- Keep one weekday completely market-free. Phone off, charts closed, not a peek.
- Cap online trading-community time. Set an explicit weekly limit and treat it like any other discretionary screen time.
- Invest in face-to-face relationships actively. Book the dinner. Send the message. Make the visit.
- If trading has progressively crowded out everything else, treat that as a clinical signal, not a lifestyle. The pattern matches addiction more closely than freedom.

Why the body needs other people

Loneliness is not just an unpleasant feeling. Research over decades has shown that chronic social isolation is an independent risk factor for cardiovascular disease, cognitive decline, and shortened life expectancy. The size of the effect is comparable to well-known physical risks like smoking. The mechanisms are partly behavioral — lonely people exercise less, sleep worse, eat differently — and partly direct, through the chronic stress chemistry that prolonged isolation activates.

A trading life that systematically removes the trader from face-to-face contact for most working hours is not a neutral lifestyle choice. The body registers it as stress, and over years, the stress shows up. The loneliness does not feel dramatic in any single week. It accumulates.

What actually counts as a real relationship

An online community organized around a shared activity is real in some respects. People are present. Conversation happens. But the relationships have a property that face-to-face friendships do not: they are mediated by the activity. Step away from the activity, and the community recedes. The friendships of someone who quit trading two years ago do not visit when you are sick, attend the wedding, or help with the move. Friendships built across decades of shared, in-person life do.

This is not a criticism of online community. It is a recognition that one does not substitute for the other. A healthy life almost certainly contains both. A life in which the only community is online, and the only shared activity is staring at price charts, has a thin layer of connection where a thick one used to be.

The weekly market-free day

One of the cheapest, most reliable defenses against trading-induced isolation is a weekly day with no markets at all. Phone away from the bedroom. Charts not opened. Trading apps deleted from the lock screen. Whatever the day contains, it is not trading. The point is not to be virtuous. The point is to remind the body and the brain that there is a life outside the screen.

Most traders who try this discover something they did not expect. They sleep better that night. They feel calmer the next morning. The week that follows is more productive, not less. The market does not punish them for the absence. The hours they would have spent monitoring positions that did not need monitoring become hours spent on a walk, a meal, a friend, a book. Those hours, accumulated across years, are most of what a life is made of.

Three small habits that protect connection

- A standing weekly phone call with someone who matters to you and who has nothing to do with markets. Same time each week. Forty-five minutes. No checking the phone during it.
- A monthly in-person meal with a friend or small group. The economy of attention required to be present at a real meal, with real conversation, exercises a muscle that screen relationships do not.
- A daily ritual with the people you live with, however small. A morning conversation. Dinner. A walk. The point is not the activity. The point is that something happens every day that is shared, present, and not mediated by a screen.

These three habits cost essentially nothing and do more for long-run mental health than most paid interventions. They also push back against the gravitational pull toward isolation that comes with intensive screen-based work. A trader who keeps these habits intact has a different life from one who lets them slip. The slipping is gradual. The habits, defended deliberately, are the structure that holds.

When trading communities turn into echo chambers

Online trading communities tend to develop their own internal logic, separate from the broader world's. Members reinforce each other's views about which strategies work, which gurus are credible, which market regimes are about to begin. The reinforcement feels like community, and at one level it is. At another level, it can become an echo chamber where bad ideas survive longer than they should because everyone in the room agrees with them.

The defense is to maintain meaningful contact with people outside the trading community — friends who do not trade, family members who would rather talk about something else, colleagues whose conversations are about anything other than markets. These outside connections provide a reality check that the community cannot. They notice when the trader's focus on markets has become unhealthy, when the language has shifted, when the priorities have drifted. The trader who only socializes inside the community has no early-warning system. The trader who maintains balance has one.

How small social rituals add up

Small, regular social rituals — a weekly meal with friends, a monthly outing, a daily ten-minute conversation with a neighbor — are dramatically more protective against isolation than people expect. Each instance is small. The cumulative effect, across a year, is a network of human contact that holds even when the rest of life gets hard.

The trader who tells themselves they will socialize "when things calm down" almost always finds that things never calm down enough. The protective rituals exist precisely because they happen regardless of how busy or stressed the trader feels. They are calendar items, not optional ones. The trader who treats them that way maintains a social life across years of intense work. The trader who treats them as flexible loses them gradually, often without noticing, and ends up isolated in ways that are hard to reverse later.

What is left when trading stops

A trader who quits day trading often finds, in the first weeks, that life feels strange. The hours that were filled with screens are now empty. The dopamine cycles that came with each trade are gone. The community that was organized around trading is no longer relevant. The strangeness is real and uncomfortable, and it is also temporary.

Most former traders, looking back, describe what came next as one of the surprises of recovery. They expected the absence to be a gap. It turned out to be space. Space for sleep, for exercise, for friends, for hobbies, for the family they had been half-present with. The space did not stay empty. It filled with the parts of life that trading had been crowding out. The reader contemplating quitting should know that the post-trading life is not a diminished version of the trading life. It is, for most former traders, a fuller one. The transition is uncomfortable. The destination is good.

Why a single weekly anchor matters

If only one social commitment can be defended each week, the most useful one for someone working alone is a recurring face-to-face appointment with a person who matters: a meal with a friend, a walk with a sibling, a coffee with a former colleague. Same time each week, scheduled on the calendar, treated as non-negotiable. The point is the anchor more than any specific conversation. The anchor pulls the rest of the week into shape around it. Without an anchor, weeks drift into each other and isolation builds quietly. With one, there is at least one moment per week where the trader is reminded that a life outside the screen exists and is worth showing up for.

> *Markets do not love you back. People can.*
> *Allocate accordingly.*

Chapter 18

Drug Addiction and Substance Abuse

Substance use among active retail traders is widespread enough, and damaging enough, that it deserves a chapter rather than a paragraph. The pattern is not universal — many traders use no substances at all — but the population-level rates are elevated, and the interaction between substances and trading produces feedback loops that compound the harm of each.

Why the rates are higher

Three structural features of the trading life raise the probability of substance use:

- Stress without recovery. Chronic activation of the stress response is a known risk factor for self-medicating with alcohol, cannabis, and benzodiazepines.
- Performance pressure. A recognized risk factor for stimulant use among professionals in cognitively demanding jobs, from finance to medicine to academia.
- Social isolation. A strong independent correlate of escalating use, because there are no co-located observers to notice the trajectory and intervene.

Alcohol

The most common pattern. The trader has a difficult session and unwinds with a drink at the close. The single drink becomes two. Two becomes a routine. Tolerance rises gradually. Daily use becomes the norm. The trader tells themselves the alcohol is recreation; the body and the bank account record it as a coping mechanism. Validated screening instruments — AUDIT, CAGE — are free, take five minutes, and can be self-administered. Any trader uncertain about the trajectory of their drinking can get a useful answer from one before lunch.

Cannabis

In jurisdictions where cannabis is legal, daily use among retail traders is reported with notable frequency. Subjectively, users describe it as helping them sit through losses and tolerate the boredom between trades. Objectively, the impact on working memory, executive function, and motivation in regular daily users is well documented in the medical literature. A trader who needs cannabis to tolerate the activity has a useful diagnostic signal: the activity is not appropriate at its current intensity.

Stimulants

Prescription stimulants — Adderall, Vyvanse, modafinil — circulate within trading communities both legally and through diversion. Short-term, they produce subjective focus and willingness to sit at the screen. Medium-term, they degrade sleep, raise blood pressure, and produce dependency. Long-term, the cardiovascular effects of chronic stimulant use, especially without clinical monitoring, are real. The medical literature is mature. The trading-community discussion of it is not.

Sedatives and benzodiazepines

On the other end of the chemistry spectrum, sedatives are sometimes used to manage post-session anxiety and insomnia. Benzodiazepines are exceptionally addictive and produce dangerous withdrawal syndromes. Any trader using them daily without clinical supervision is in territory where consultation with a physician is urgent rather than optional.

Caffeine and nicotine

Nicotine vaping has become common among younger retail traders. Subjectively, users report focus benefits. Objectively, nicotine is a vasoconstrictor and a documented risk factor for heart disease. Caffeine in moderate doses is fine for most people. In the multi-cup, late-afternoon doses common among traders, it interacts with sleep and anxiety in counterproductive ways.

The interaction with money decisions

Substances impair the cognitive functions trading most depends on: working memory, impulse control, accurate probability assessment, and recognition of escalating commitment to losing positions. A trader making real-money decisions while impaired is making them poorly. The cost is not abstract. Specific traders reading this chapter are paying it right now.

What to do

- Be honest with yourself, on paper, about current use frequency and trend over the last year.
- Self-administer a validated screening instrument — AUDIT for alcohol, ASSIST for general substances. The instruments are free, fast, and useful.
- Discuss the result with a physician or a licensed mental-health professional. Honest disclosure to a

clinician is protected and useful.

- Recognize that substance use and active trading reinforce each other. Treating either alone is harder than treating both together.

The functional user

Functional users — those whose substance use is regular but does not yet cause visible problems at work or in relationships — are the population most likely to delay getting help. The functioning is partial protection, but it is also partial concealment. The visible impairment that prompts intervention in others has not yet appeared. Internal markers, however, often have: degraded sleep, blunted emotional range, a sense that the day requires the substance to be tolerable, the recognition that the substance has moved from optional to required.

These internal markers are more sensitive than external impairment, and worth taking seriously even before the external signs arrive. A trader who notices any of them honestly is not in trouble yet, but is on a trajectory that gets harder to change the longer it continues.

Why trading and substances reinforce each other

Substance use does not just emerge from trading stress. It also makes trading worse. Alcohol degrades judgment, working memory, and impulse control — all faculties that trading depends on. Cannabis impairs working memory and motivation. Stimulants produce overconfidence and willingness to take risks the trader would not normally take. Benzodiazepines impair memory consolidation, making it harder to learn from past mistakes.

The trader using substances is making real-money decisions in a degraded state, and the decisions are predictably worse. The losses produced by the impaired decisions then drive more substance use to manage the resulting stress. The loop reinforces itself. Treating either the trading or the substance use alone is harder than treating both together.

How to ask for help

Asking for help with substance use is one of the harder things a person can do. The shame of admitting the problem combines with the fear of what will happen next — losing the substance, losing the trading, losing the privacy of the household — to keep most people silent for longer than they should be.

The honest first step is usually the smallest one. A self-administered screening tool (AUDIT for alcohol, ASSIST for general substance use) takes a few minutes and gives an objective indication of whether use is in concerning territory. A primary-care physician can review the result and refer to specialists if needed. The conversation is confidential and does not lead to immediate consequences in most cases. The trader who takes that small first step has done something nine out of ten people in the same situation never do, and has bought themselves the chance of a different outcome.

Why standard advice does not work for everyone

Standard advice for substance use — "drink less," "cut back," "try moderation" — works for some people and fails for others. For some, the relationship with a substance is fundamentally different from social drinking or occasional use. The substance has become a coping mechanism, a regulator of mood, a partner in the daily routine. Cutting back through willpower works only briefly; the use returns to its previous level within weeks.

If standard advice has not worked, the next step is not to try harder. It is to get specialized help. Addiction medicine has matured significantly in recent decades. Effective medications exist for alcohol use disorder, opioid use disorder, and tobacco dependence. Specialized counseling protocols address behavioral patterns that pure willpower cannot. A primary-care physician can refer to specialists, and many employers offer confidential employee assistance programs that cover the initial visits. The first step is harder than the rest. The first step is also the one that makes the rest possible.

Why early help matters most

Substance use disorders, like many medical conditions, are easier to treat early than late. The patterns are less established. The neurochemical changes are less entrenched. The social structures around the substance — the friends who use, the routines that include it, the rituals that depend on it — are less calcified. Early intervention reaches a person whose life is mostly intact, whose relationships are mostly healthy, whose career is mostly on track. Late intervention reaches a person who has lost more, and recovery has more ground to recover.

The signal that suggests early help would be useful is simple: you have privately considered, more than once, that your use might have crossed a line. That private consideration is rarely wrong. People without an emerging problem do not have it. The reader who has had that thought has already gathered the most important diagnostic information themselves. The next step is a conversation with a clinician, which is confidential, low-risk, and capable of producing answers that a quiet self-evaluation cannot.

When work-related substance use is normalized

In some industries, regular alcohol or stimulant use is treated as part of the work culture. Finance has historically been one of those industries. The drink at the close. The performance-enhancing substance during a stressful project. The shared smoke during the break. Each of these can feel normal in context, even when they would not be normal in another setting.

Normalization is not the same as safety. The substance does not know it is part of a culture. Its effects on the body and the mind are the same whether it is consumed alone in shame or with colleagues at an office event. A reader whose use has scaled up because the surrounding culture supports it should know that the cultural context will not be there at the lab work, in the relationship strain, in the impaired decisions. The body keeps its own record.

Why combined treatment usually works better

When trading and substance use are present together, treating either one alone is harder than treating both together. Each pattern reinforces the other. The trader who quits the substance while continuing to trade often relapses, because the trading provides the stress that drove the substance use to begin with. The trader who quits trading while continuing to use heavily often does not quit trading durably, because the impaired decision-making that comes with substance use makes returning to the activity easier than it should be.

Specialized treatment programs that address both behaviors together produce better outcomes than treatment of either alone. The reader struggling with both should look specifically for clinicians or programs that have experience with this combination, rather than picking a generalist for one and hoping the other will resolve on its own. The combination is common. The treatment is increasingly recognized. Asking for it specifically is not a strange request.

Why the first conversation is worth its weight

If substance use has become a quiet presence in a trading life, the single most useful action is the first honest conversation with a clinician. The conversation is short. The clinician has heard versions of the same story from many other patients. They will not be alarmed. They will ask straightforward questions, listen, and propose next steps appropriate to what they hear. The reader who imagines the conversation as dramatic is usually surprised by how ordinary it actually is. The drama lives in the avoidance, not in the talking.

> *The substances that make trading tolerable are evidence that the trading is not.*

Chapter 19

Day Trading Addiction

Behavioral addiction is a recognized clinical phenomenon. Gambling disorder is in the standard diagnostic manuals as a non-substance addictive disorder, with diagnostic criteria, validated screening instruments, and established treatment pathways. Day trading, when it presents the relevant pattern, fits cleanly inside the behavioral-addiction framework. This chapter sets out the criteria honestly and explains what the framework implies.

The pattern

Adapting the standard gambling-disorder criteria to trading, the relevant pattern includes:

- Preoccupation: persistent thoughts about trading, planning the next session, replaying past trades.
- Tolerance: needing larger size, more frequency, or more leverage to feel the same engagement.
- Withdrawal-like symptoms: restlessness or irritability when not able to trade.
- Loss of control: repeated unsuccessful attempts to cut back.
- Chasing losses: returning to the screen to recover prior losses, often with larger positions.
- Lying or concealment: hiding the extent of trading from family or financial advisors.
- Functional impairment: jeopardizing relationships, work, education, or finances because of trading.
- Reliance on others: borrowing money or relying on others to relieve trading-related financial problems.

Meeting four or more of these criteria over a twelve-month period would, in clinical assessment of analogous gambling behavior, justify the disorder diagnosis. Not all traders meet the criteria. Some who think they do not, do.

Why the schedule is so addictive

Behavioral psychology established decades ago that variable-ratio reinforcement — rewards arriving unpredictably and at irregular intervals — produces the most persistent operant behavior known. Slot machines are engineered around this schedule. Day trading delivers a near-perfect implementation of the same schedule. Most attempts produce nothing or small losses. Occasional attempts produce vivid wins. The timing of the wins is unpredictable. The activity hijacks the same brain circuits that gambling and substance use hijack, with the additional feature of being socially endorsed and dressed in the language of business.

App design is on the other side

Modern trading apps are designed to maximize engagement. Push notifications about price moves and account changes. Confetti animations on trade execution. Gamified streak features. Levels, badges, social leaderboards. None of these features improve the user's outcomes. All of them increase screen time and trade frequency. The platforms know what they are doing. Class-action lawsuits, regulatory inquiries, and academic research have documented it.

The progression

A typical addiction trajectory in trading begins with curiosity, accelerates through small early wins (the "beginner's-luck" phase that recruits engagement), continues through a plateau of mixed results, and progresses to compensatory escalation: more time, more capital, more leverage, more risk taken to recover from losses or recapture the early thrill. The terminal stages involve substantial financial harm, hidden borrowing, deteriorating relationships, and the secrecy that marks any serious behavioral addiction.

Recovery

Recovery resembles other behavioral-addiction recoveries. Honest assessment. Professional support. Structural barriers — closed accounts, deleted apps, limited access to capital. Peer support, including Gamblers Anonymous and a growing number of trading-specific recovery communities. Sustained reduction in time spent in the triggering environment. Cognitive-behavioral therapy has documented effectiveness. The process is real, takes time, and is well worth doing.

The hardest part

The hardest part, for most traders, is the identity reset. Quitting trading is not just losing an activity; it is losing a story the trader has told about themselves, often for years. "I was going to make it." "I was almost there." "This time would have been different." Therapists who work with recovering traders consistently report that the financial reset is easier than the identity reset. The good news is that other identities are available. Investor, parent, professional, friend — each is more durable than "trader," and most of them are in better long-run alignment with the trader's actual underlying goals.

The slot-machine design of trading apps

Modern trading apps are not neutral interfaces for accessing markets. They are products designed by teams of designers, behavioral psychologists, and engineers whose performance is measured by how engaged users are. Engagement, in their terminology, means how often users open the app, how long they stay in it, and how many actions they take while there. None of these metrics correspond to user financial outcomes.

The design choices follow from the metrics. Push notifications about price moves and account changes. Confetti animations on trade execution. Color-coded charts that pulse with movement. Streak indicators. Levels and badges. Social leaderboards. Gestures that make placing a trade as fluid as scrolling through photos. Every one of these features increases engagement. Almost none of them improves outcomes. The platforms know what they are doing. Class-action lawsuits, regulatory inquiries, and academic research have documented it across multiple jurisdictions.

Why willpower runs out

Behavioral research has shown clearly that willpower is a finite resource. The same person who easily resists temptation in the morning, when rested, struggles to resist the same temptation in the evening, when tired. Willpower depletes through use, like a muscle. The trader who has been making decisions under pressure for six straight hours is operating with less willpower than they had at the start of the day, even if they do not feel it.

This is why discipline alone does not protect against trading addiction. The trader is not in a fair fight. They are competing against an environment designed to exhaust their self-control, with a brain whose self-control depletes through use, and at exactly the moments when their self-control is weakest, the environment is loudest. The honest defense is structural — fewer apps, lower account sizes, automated rules, accountability partners, real distance between the trader and the screen.

Recovery looks like other recoveries

Recovery from trading addiction follows the same shape as recovery from other behavioral addictions. The first weeks are dominated by urges to check, by withdrawal-like symptoms (restlessness, irritability, intrusive thoughts about positions), and by a strange empty feeling at session times. These symptoms attenuate over weeks, not days. Most former active traders report that the first month is the hardest, the third month is the inflection, and the second year is the moment they realize how much of life had been crowded out and how much returned once the activity stepped back.

The recovery is real and worth doing. It is also not always linear. Relapses are common and do not mean recovery has failed. They mean the path is longer than the trader hoped, and the structural protections need to be strengthened. A therapist familiar with behavioral addictions, a peer-support group, or both, dramatically increase the probability of a durable outcome. None of this is a sign of weakness. It is the basic infrastructure of changing a deeply established pattern of behavior.

What relapse means and what it does not

Recovery from any behavioral addiction is rarely linear. A trader who has stopped for several months may find themselves logging back into a brokerage account during a stressful week, taking a few small positions, telling themselves it is fine. This is a relapse. It does not mean recovery has failed. It means the path is longer than the trader hoped, and the structural protections need to be strengthened.

What relapse does not mean is that the trader is incapable of changing. The vast majority of people who eventually achieve durable recovery from behavioral addictions experienced multiple relapses along the way. The pattern is the rule, not the exception. A trader who relapses and treats it as evidence of personal failure is more likely to spiral. A trader who relapses and treats it as information — about which protections were inadequate, which triggers were not anticipated, which support systems need strengthening — is more likely to come out the other side.

What an identity reset actually looks like

The hardest part of leaving trading, for many former traders, is not the financial reset. It is the identity reset. "I was a trader" was a story they told themselves and others for years. Letting it go feels like loss. The good news is that other identities are available, and most of them serve the trader's actual underlying goals better. Investor. Parent. Spouse. Professional in the field where they earn a living. Friend. Each of these is more durable than "trader," and each compounds across decades in ways that trading does not.

The reset usually happens slowly. The trader stops checking trading apps that have been deleted. They notice they have more time. They reinvest the time in something else — work, a hobby, family, exercise. After a year or two, when they look back, the trading identity has receded into something they used to do, rather than something they are. The story has changed. The change happened by living differently, not by deciding differently.

Why hiding accelerates harm

Behavioral addictions tend to escalate when they are hidden and to slow or reverse when they are not. The reasons are practical. A hidden activity does not face the social friction that would normally constrain it. There are no questions from family. No accountability conversations. No external observer noticing patterns the practitioner cannot see in themselves.

Once the activity becomes visible — to a partner, a therapist, a peer-support group — the same activity faces friction it never faced before. Choices that were easy in private are harder to make in public. Patterns that escalated in silence often slow when they are seen. This is why the simplest single intervention for behavioral addiction, including trading, is to make the activity visible to at least one trusted person. Doing so does not solve the problem. It changes the conditions in which the problem operates, in ways that increase the chance of recovery.

Why support groups work

Peer support groups for behavioral addictions — whether the addiction is gambling, gaming, shopping, or trading — have a measurable effect on outcomes. The mechanism is not mysterious. People in the group are at different stages of recovery. Newer members benefit from the experience of those further along. Longer-term members benefit from articulating their own experience to newer ones. The shared honesty about a condition that is otherwise secret reduces shame, which reduces relapse risk.

Many cities have Gamblers Anonymous chapters that explicitly include trading-related compulsive behavior. Online versions exist for readers in places where in-person groups are not available. Joining is free. The first meeting is the hardest, in the same way that the first conversation about hidden trading with a partner is hard. After the first meeting, returning is much easier. Many people in long-term recovery from trading-related compulsive behavior credit a peer support group as the most helpful single intervention they participated in. It costs nothing and works in ways that paid services often do not.

Why the diagnosis itself helps

For some readers, simply recognizing that their pattern fits the diagnostic criteria for behavioral addiction is the most important moment in the recovery. Up until that moment, the trader has been telling themselves they have a personal problem with discipline, character, or strategy. The problem feels private and shameful. After the moment, the trader sees that they have a recognized condition with established treatments, support communities, and predictable trajectories. The shame does not disappear, but it changes shape. The condition is not a personal flaw; it is a clinical pattern that has affected millions of people.

This reframing matters because it makes the next steps easier. Treatments exist. Support groups exist. Other people have walked the same path and come out the other side. The reader is not the only person to have ended up here, and they will not be the last. The condition has a name. The path forward has a shape. Recognizing both is the work of the diagnosis, and the recognition itself is one of the most useful things that can happen.

Why naming the pattern matters

There is a quiet relief in being able to name what is happening. For months or years, the trader has felt that something is wrong without having a clear word for it. Naming the pattern as behavioral addiction does not make it pleasant, but it does make it legible. The trader sees that they are not uniquely defective, not uniquely weak, not uniquely failing at something everyone else is succeeding at. They are inside a recognized condition that has produced the same pattern in many other people, and that has a documented path of recovery that has worked for others. The relief of legibility is itself part of how recovery begins.

If you cannot stop, the activity is no longer a choice. That is the diagnostic. Treat it accordingly.

Chapter 20

Discipline and Risk Management

Risk management is the part of trading that almost everyone says they take seriously and almost no one actually practices. The standard rules are well known and almost never enforced. This chapter sets them out plainly and then explains why discipline alone, even when it works, is not enough.

Risk per trade

The first rule, used by serious practitioners across markets, is to risk a small fixed fraction of equity on any single trade. One percent is conservative. Two percent is the upper end of widely cited guidance. Risk is defined as the dollar distance from entry price to stop-loss price, multiplied by position size. A trader with a twenty-thousand-dollar account, applying a one-percent rule, risks two hundred dollars per trade.

The math then dictates position size. Suppose you want to buy a stock at fifty dollars with a stop at forty-eight. Your risk per share is two dollars. Two hundred dollars divided by two dollars equals one hundred shares. The notional position is five thousand dollars. The discipline is to follow the math and resist taking a larger position because the calculated size feels "too small to be worth it."

Risk across the portfolio

Per-trade risk is necessary but not sufficient. A trader who sizes each individual position correctly but holds five correlated positions simultaneously is running effectively one bigger position, not five small ones. Sector concentration, similar size factors, similar themes — all reduce the diversification a per-trade rule appears to deliver. Honest portfolio risk management caps total open exposure at some multiple of the per-trade limit and limits sector concentration deliberately.

Daily and weekly stops

Professionals use hard daily and weekly loss limits. If the day's losses reach a defined dollar amount or percent of equity, trading stops for the day. If the week's losses reach a defined level, trading stops for the week. The mechanism that makes this work is structural enforcement: the broker, an external accountability partner, or an account configuration that simply does not let the trader place new orders. Pure willpower does not reliably enforce these rules during a stressed session, because willpower is the resource the session is depleting.

Stops are not insurance

A stop-loss is a market order triggered at a price level. In fast markets, gaps, halts, or thin liquidity can produce fills meaningfully worse than the trigger. Stops are useful tools for limiting expected losses. They are not a guarantee. The trader who treats them as a guarantee will eventually be surprised by an exception.

Why discipline is not enough

Suppose a trader has perfect discipline. They size every trade correctly, honor every stop, take every break the rules require. If the underlying strategy has zero or negative expected value after costs, the trader still loses money — just more slowly and elegantly than a sloppier counterpart. Risk management answers the question, "given a positive edge, how do I avoid blowing up before the edge plays out." It does not answer the prior question, "do I have a positive edge to begin with, after costs, in the regime I'm trading in." Most retail strategies fail the prior question.

The honest measurement

- Track every trade. Date, time, instrument, entry, exit, size, and result after costs.
- Compute realized win rate, average win, average loss, and net expectancy after at least a hundred trades.
- Demand a sample size of at least a hundred trades before drawing any conclusion. Demand five hundred before claiming statistical confidence.
- If the math shows negative expectancy, do not adjust the strategy to keep trading. Stop. Adjusting to maintain activity is a behavioral pattern, not a strategy improvement.

What survives over time

Successful long-term traders, when asked about their edge, rarely say "I read charts better than anyone else." They say some version of "I survive bad runs and stay in the game." Survival is achieved through structure: small per-trade risk, low correlation, ample reserve capital, no leverage in early years, and willingness to step away. Survival without an underlying edge is a long, slow loss. Survival with an edge produces compounding. Either way, survival comes first.

Daily and weekly stop rules

Professional traders use hard daily and weekly loss limits as a basic structural defense. The rule is straightforward: if the day's losses reach a defined dollar amount or percent of equity, trading stops for the day. If the week's losses reach a defined level, trading stops for the week. The amounts are decided in advance, when the trader is calm, and enforced by structure rather than willpower.

The mechanism that makes this work is automation. The broker can be configured to block new trades after a defined daily loss. An accountability partner can hold a credential that locks the account. The trader's spouse can know the rule and ask about it. Whatever the structure, the point is that the decision to stop is made once, while calm, and applied automatically when needed. Pure willpower does not enforce these rules during a stressed session, because willpower is exactly the resource the session is depleting.

The 'just one more trade' trap

A common pattern: the trader has hit their daily loss limit. They tell themselves they will stop. They watch the market. They see what they consider an obvious setup. They take "just one more trade." The trade frequently makes the loss worse. The phenomenon is not weakness. It is the predictable result of the addictive design of trading and the cognitive degradation that accompanies losses.

The protective behavior is to recognize that the urge to take "just one more trade" is itself a signal that no trade should be taken. The trader is in the cognitive state most likely to compound the loss. Stop. Walk away. Eat a meal. Sleep. Re-enter the market only when calm, and only on the next allowed session.

The revenge trade

The most dangerous trade in a trader's career is the one taken to recover from a large loss. The trade is sized larger than the rules allow, taken in markets the trader does not normally trade, with conviction that exceeds the evidence. The arithmetic of recovery — needing a one hundred percent gain to recover from a fifty percent drawdown — combines with the trader's emotional state to produce decisions that look reasonable in the moment and disastrous in retrospect.

The empirical pattern is so consistent that recovering traders refer to it by name: the revenge trade. The protective behavior is to recognize the urge as a signal of impaired decision-making and step away. Hours, not minutes. Days, not hours. The market will be there when the trader returns to it calm. The position they were tempted to take will not have changed enough to matter. The trader's state will.

What edge looks like, honestly

A real edge is small, hard-won, and difficult to identify with confidence over short samples. A strategy that produces an honest expectancy of, say, fifty cents per round trip after costs is a meaningful edge. It is also barely visible in a sample of ten or twenty trades; the noise drowns out the signal. To have any statistical confidence that the edge is real, the trader needs hundreds of trades, ideally thousands, executed under the same rules in similar market conditions.

Most retail traders never accumulate that kind of sample. They switch strategies, change instruments, take breaks, alter position sizes. Each change resets the count. They end up with a small handful of trades under any single approach, and the small handful is almost entirely noise. They cannot tell whether they have an edge or are just lucky, and that uncertainty is the most dangerous regime to size positions in.

Why most risk-management rules fail in practice

Almost every retail trader, asked about risk management, can recite the standard rules: small per-trade risk, stop-losses on every position, daily and weekly loss limits, reduced size after losses. Almost none of them follow the rules consistently. The gap between knowing and doing is the central problem of trading psychology, and willpower alone does not close it.

What does close it is structure. Limits enforced by the broker rather than the trader. Position-size calculators built into the trading interface. Account configurations that prevent trades larger than a defined size. Accountability partners who review the trading log weekly. Smaller account sizes that mathematically prevent the worst outcomes. The trader who builds these structures while calm and rested is delegating decisions to a system that does not get tired. The trader relying on willpower at 3 p.m. on a losing day is delegating decisions to the most unreliable version of themselves.

The math of recovery

When a trader is in a drawdown, the urge to take larger trades to recover is strong. The math, however, runs the wrong way. Suppose a trader has taken a thirty percent drawdown. To return to even, they need a forty-three percent gain on what is left. That is a substantial gain to demand from any strategy. Doubling the position size to try to get there faster also doubles the volatility, which means another adverse stretch can produce a much deeper drawdown than the original — fifty or sixty percent.

The honest path back from a drawdown is the slow one. Reduce position size, not increase it. Trade less frequently, not more. Examine why the drawdown happened and adjust the strategy, accepting that the next year may not produce a heroic recovery. Many traders end careers in the moment they decided that the heroic recovery was the only acceptable response to the drawdown. The slow path is less dramatic and dramatically more likely to result in actual recovery.

Why most rules are broken in the same way

When traders break their own risk-management rules, the breaks tend to follow a small number of recognizable patterns. The position is held past the stop because "this time the stop is too tight." The size is increased beyond the limit because "this setup is unusually clear." The daily loss limit is overridden because "the market is finally showing me what I expected." In each case, the trader has constructed a story that justifies the exception, and the story sounds reasonable in the moment.

The reasonable-sounding stories are the warning sign. A risk-management rule that is occasionally broken with good reason is not a rule; it is a guideline. The honest test is whether the rule is followed even when the trader has a story for breaking it. If the answer is yes, the rule is real. If the answer is no, the trader has not actually committed to risk management; they have committed to risk management when convenient. The market does not care about convenience.

What separates rules from guidelines

A rule, in trading, is something that is followed regardless of how the trader feels in the moment. A guideline is something that is followed when convenient and abandoned when not. Most retail traders write rules and follow guidelines. They tell themselves the difference does not matter much. It does.

Rules followed consistently over time produce predictable outcomes. The trader can analyze whether the strategy works, because the data reflects what the strategy actually does. Guidelines followed inconsistently produce data that reflects nothing in particular. The trader cannot tell whether the strategy is good, because the strategy was not actually executed. Most retail traders are evaluating guidelines and concluding things about strategies. The conclusions are unreliable. The discipline of converting guidelines into rules — by enforcing them structurally rather than by willpower — is the difference between actually testing a strategy and pretending to.

Why annual review is more useful than monthly

Many trading books recommend frequent review — daily journals, weekly performance reviews, monthly strategy meetings with yourself. The frequent reviews do less than they promise. The sample size in any given month is too small to distinguish skill from luck. Decisions made in response to monthly results often add noise rather than signal.

An annual review, by contrast, includes enough trades and enough market conditions that real patterns can be seen. The annual review asks: did the strategy work, after all costs and taxes? Did I follow my rules? What did I learn about myself? What needs to change for next year? The answers are more reliable than monthly reviews would produce, and the review does not tempt the trader to over-adjust based on short-term noise. The trader who reviews annually and otherwise leaves the strategy alone is borrowing the patience of a long-term investor for the structure of their trading life.

Why writing it down is most of the discipline

A surprising amount of trading discipline comes from one habit: writing things down. Writing the trading plan down before the day starts. Writing the rationale for each trade before placing it. Writing the result after closing it. Writing the weekly review of what worked and what did not. Writing the annual evaluation of whether the strategy is producing what it is supposed to.

Each of these is a small act. Cumulatively, they replace the trader's vague memory of what they were doing with a written record they can examine. The written record is harder to lie to than memory. It surfaces patterns that intuition misses. It catches drift early, while there is still time to correct it. The trader who writes everything down is borrowing the structure of a professional process for an activity that, in retail, is usually done without any structure at all. The borrowed structure is one of the cheapest improvements a retail trader can make to their own results.

> *Discipline is necessary. It is not sufficient. The market does not give credit for elegant losing.*

Chapter 21

Day Trading Versus Gambling

Comparing day trading to gambling makes traders defensive. The defense usually includes some version of "this is skill, not luck." The honest answer is that the comparison is closer than the trader wants and farther than the casino owner wants. The structural similarities and the meaningful differences both deserve clear treatment.

Where the two activities overlap

- Both involve risking capital on uncertain short-term outcomes.
- Both rely on a variable-ratio reinforcement schedule, which is the most addictive pattern known to behavioral psychology.
- Both feature a population in which the median participant loses to a small minority of consistent winners and to the house.
- Both feature aggressive marketing that emphasizes the winners and obscures the losers.
- Both produce documented behavioral-addiction patterns in a substantial minority of participants.
- Both are venues where social isolation, financial stress, and substance use accelerate harm.

Where the two activities differ

Casino games have a fixed, calculable house edge. Trading does not have a single fixed edge; the cost to the participant depends on the strategy, the market, the venue, and the participant's behavior. Some narrow trading strategies have positive expected value for skilled implementers. No casino game does, for the player.

Casino games are pure stochastic processes within their rules. Markets aggregate the actions of millions of participants and reflect real economic information. A small minority of traders can develop genuine, durable edges based on superior information processing or specialized infrastructure. The minority is small, the path is narrow, and almost no participant on a retail trading app is in it. The fact that the path exists is sometimes used to justify continued participation by people who are not on it.

Long-term investing is fundamentally different from both gambling and day trading. The long-term investor in productive assets is paid by the cash flows of those assets over years. The expected return is positive, the path can be modeled, and the strategy does not require outwitting other participants. This is the most important distinction the casino comparison sometimes obscures: not all market activities are gambling. Day trading is closer to gambling than long-term investing is.

What gambling research teaches

Decades of work on gambling addiction has produced robust findings that apply directly to trading. Early wins predict longer engagement. Loss-chasing is the strongest single predictor of escalation. Cognitive distortions — "I am due," "this time will be different" — cluster around losses. Continuous-availability formats, like online slots and in-play sports betting, produce more harm than scheduled formats. Day trading is the financial equivalent of continuous-availability gambling: open during all market hours, on a phone, with one-click execution and a constantly updating leaderboard.

What regulators say

U.S. regulators do not officially label day trading as gambling, but their consumer-facing communications use language that reflects the substantial overlap. FINRA's Day-Trading Risk Disclosure rule requires firms to inform clients that day trading is "extremely risky," that the typical day trader will "suffer severe financial losses," and that they should not use funds they cannot afford to lose. The SEC's investor-education page on day trading includes the same warnings, framed in plain language. These are not casual disclaimers. They are the regulators' distilled conclusion from decades of investor harm.

The practical implication

Treating day trading as a category similar to recreational gambling has practical consequences. The dollars involved should be dollars the household can afford to lose. The time involved should be time the household can spare. The activity should not be funded by leverage, by debt, or by money belonging to other goals. It should not crowd out the long-term investing that builds real wealth. The trader should be honest about whether the activity is producing the hobby satisfaction recreational gambling can plausibly produce, or instead the harm pattern pathological gambling reliably produces.

What gambling researchers have already learned

Decades of work on gambling addiction has produced findings that apply directly to trading. Early wins predict longer engagement, because the early winner concludes they have a real edge when they were mostly lucky. Loss-chasing — placing larger bets to recover prior losses — is the strongest single predictor of escalation toward severe harm. Continuous-availability formats produce more harm than scheduled formats. The gambler who can only play once a week is in much less danger than the one who can play whenever the urge strikes.

Day trading on a phone, with one-click execution and a constantly updating leaderboard of names you could trade right now, is the financial equivalent of continuous-availability gambling. The format is the most harmful one identified in gambling research, applied to a market that does not call itself gambling and does not come with the consumer protections that regulated gambling does.

What being honest with yourself looks like

A useful exercise: pretend, for a moment, that day trading is gambling. Apply the rules a thoughtful person would apply to recreational gambling. Use only money you can afford to lose. Set a hard budget. Stop when the budget is gone. Do not chase losses. Do not borrow. Do not let the activity interfere with work, family, or sleep. Tell your partner the actual numbers.

If, applying those rules, the activity still feels worthwhile to you as a hobby, you have framed it accurately. If, applying those rules, the activity stops being worthwhile, you have learned something important about why you were doing it. The rules do not change the nature of the activity. They just make the nature of the activity visible.

What casinos know that markets pretend not to

Regulated casinos in most jurisdictions are required to make certain disclosures: the house edge for various games, responsible-gambling resources, the option for self-exclusion. The disclosures exist because, after observing what happens to a non-trivial minority of gamblers, regulators decided that the activity required these protections.

Markets, when accessed for short-term speculation, behave more like casino games than the marketing suggests. Yet the equivalent disclosures are weaker. There is no required disclosure that the typical short-term retail trader loses money. There is no automatic self-exclusion option for traders who recognize a problem in themselves. The structural similarity to gambling is real; the regulatory response has not yet caught up. A reader who recognizes this can apply gambling-style protections to themselves voluntarily, even without the formal infrastructure to enforce them.

Self-exclusion as a financial tool

Many gambling jurisdictions offer a self-exclusion program, in which an individual voluntarily bans themselves from gambling venues for a period of months or years. The mechanism removes the moment-by-moment decision from the impaired individual and hands it to a structural barrier. The mechanism works precisely because it does not depend on willpower at the moment of temptation.

Trading does not have an equivalent formal program, but informal versions exist. Closing brokerage accounts. Asking a partner to hold the password to any remaining accounts. Using account configurations that prevent new orders. Working with a fee-only advisor who has signature authority over investment changes. Each of these is a voluntary self-exclusion from the activity that may be causing harm. The trader who recognizes a problem and wants to stop should consider whether one of these structural barriers, not willpower alone, will be required to make the stop stick.

What treating it as a hobby looks like

If a reader, after considering everything in this book, decides to participate in day trading as a hobby — sized small, walled off, accepted as recreation rather than income — what does that actually look like in practice? A separate small account, funded with money that can be entirely lost without any household consequence. A clear weekly time budget, set in advance and not exceeded. No leverage. No connection to retirement, education, or emergency funds. No discussion of the activity as a possible career or a possible income source. No subscription to signal services, courses, or other paid products. Honest tracking of results, including the time invested, evaluated annually.

A reader who can sustain those constraints has a hobby. A reader who cannot has something else. The constraints are uncomfortable for most retail traders to hear, because they do not match the way the activity is usually marketed or experienced. They are also the constraints that turn the activity from harmful to harmless. The harmless version is real, sustainable, and compatible with a healthy life. The harmful version is what most of this book has described.

What gambling regulators have learned

Gambling regulators in many jurisdictions have, over decades, developed a reasonably effective set of consumer protections. Mandatory deposit limits. Cooling-off periods after losses. Self-exclusion programs. Public warnings about the risks. These protections exist because, after observing what happens to a non-trivial minority of gamblers without them, regulators decided that the activity required this level of structural friction.

Trading, when accessed for short-term speculation, has structural similarities to gambling that should produce similar protections. They are slowly arriving — some jurisdictions have introduced cooling-off periods on retail forex, restrictions on leverage, mandatory disclosures of percentage of clients who lose money. The trend is in the right direction. In the meantime, the reader can apply many of the same protections voluntarily — limits on deposits, cooling-off periods after losses, self-exclusion through closed accounts. The protections work as well when self-imposed as when externally enforced, as long as the structural enforcement is real.

> *If your trading is funded by money you cannot afford to lose, you are not investing. You are not even trading. You are gambling under a different name.*

Chapter 22

Crypto Currencies and Shitcoins

Major cryptocurrencies — bitcoin, ether, and a handful of others — have at least debatable long-term theses, even if those theses remain contested. Beneath the top tier sits a sea of thousands of tokens with no plausible long-term value, no working product, no durable demand, and a designed-for-promotion structure that the crypto community itself calls shitcoins. This chapter is about that lower tier, which represents most of the trading volume in retail crypto and most of the realized losses.

What "shitcoin" actually means

There is no formal definition. In practice, the label applies to tokens that share most or all of the following features:

- No working product or revenue. The token is the product.
- Concentrated insider holdings, often a majority of supply, typically vesting on schedules visible only in the project's documentation.
- A promotional ecosystem of paid influencers, paid social-media campaigns, and chat-room communities organized around price.
- Listing on a small set of cooperative exchanges, often with manipulated volume.
- A lifecycle measured in months rather than years. The chart starts at zero, peaks during the promotional cycle, and returns toward zero.
- Marketing language that conflates technological novelty with investment merit.

The math of dilution

A token launched with one billion total supply, ten percent in initial circulation and ninety percent allocated to founders and early investors with vesting schedules, has a public price reflecting only the ten percent in circulation. As vesting cliffs are reached, large blocks become liquid. Unless retail demand grows in proportion — which is almost never the case after the initial promotional cycle — the price is mechanically pressured downward. Honest review of any token's tokenomics document, before purchase, will reveal the schedule. Almost no retail buyer reads it.

Pump and dump as a recurring template

The lifecycle of a typical promoted token is well documented. Insiders accumulate cheaply. Promotional campaigns push the token to a target audience. Volume and price rise. Influencers post screenshots of paper gains. Retail buyers arrive in increasing numbers. Insiders sell into the retail demand in tranches. Volume and price collapse. The exit liquidity is the late-arriving retail. The cycle is so reliable that academic finance literature has begun classifying it formally.

Meme coins and reflexivity

Meme coins occupy a related category. They explicitly disclaim fundamental value and present themselves as collective coordination on a joke or cultural reference. A small number have produced extraordinary returns for early entrants. Many more have produced complete losses. The honest framing is that this is a lottery ticket where the participants know it is a lottery ticket, and the size of any individual position should match that framing — small, expendable, not from money meant for anything else.

Custody and venue risk

Beyond tokenomics, the venues where these tokens trade carry their own risks. Smaller exchanges have failed, frozen withdrawals, and disappeared with customer assets. Decentralized exchanges run on smart contracts that have been exploited. Wallet-based custody requires operational discipline most retail users lack. The combination of low-quality assets, fragile venues, and inexperienced users produces a risk profile that does not exist in any other corner of mainstream finance.

What a defensible crypto allocation looks like

If, after considering the risks, a reader still wants exposure to crypto as a small experimental allocation, the defensible version looks like this:

- A small percentage of net worth — small enough that a total loss is fully survivable.
- Concentrated in the largest, most liquid tokens, rather than long-tail names.
- Held with reasonable custody hygiene: hardware wallets for non-trivial amounts, regulated exchanges for amounts being actively traded, never both for the same coins.
- Approached as long-term holding rather than short-term speculation. The volatility means short-term outcomes are nearly random, while long-term outcomes are at least driven by adoption.
- Reviewed periodically with honest skepticism about whether the original thesis still holds.

Reading a tokenomics document

Every legitimate token project publishes a document — sometimes called a white paper, sometimes called a tokenomics paper — that explains how the supply is structured. The supply schedule is one of the most informative pieces of public information available, and almost no retail buyer reads it before purchasing.

The questions worth answering: How many tokens exist, total? How many are currently in circulation? Who holds the rest, and on what schedule do their holdings unlock? Are there scheduled inflation increases that will dilute existing holders? Are there mechanisms — token burns, fee redistribution — that reduce supply over time? Honest answers to these questions are usually in the document. Sometimes the answers are alarming. The day a large unlock cliff is reached is, mechanically, the day selling pressure rises and the price drops. Knowing the schedule before buying is a small effort that prevents a predictable kind of loss.

Stablecoins are not just stable

Stablecoins are tokens designed to maintain a fixed value, usually one U.S. dollar per token. They are not investments; their goal is to not appreciate. They are settlement infrastructure. The value depends entirely on what backs them. A stablecoin fully backed by short-term U.S. Treasuries and audited regularly is closer to a money-market fund. A stablecoin backed by an algorithmic mechanism, with no real reserves, is a different animal entirely.

Several algorithmic stablecoins have failed catastrophically, erasing billions of dollars within days. Some asset-backed stablecoins have proven robust through stress events. The difference matters. A reader who holds stablecoins for any reason — convenience, yield, transaction infrastructure — should know which kind they are holding and what the actual reserves look like. The information is public.

Most users do not check.

NFTs as a recent case study

Non-fungible tokens — unique tokens representing ownership of digital art, collectibles, or other items — produced a speculative wave that peaked around 2021 and largely deflated thereafter. The structural pattern matched older speculative manias: a novel technology with a real underlying idea, lifestyle imagery in marketing, celebrity endorsements, narratives about disrupting traditional markets, and a designed-for-promotion economy of creators and flippers.

Median prices for the most-traded collections fell ninety percent or more from peaks. A small number of early collectors and creators retained substantial gains. The bulk of participants paid for those gains with their own losses. The NFT cycle is a recent, well-documented example of the historical pattern of speculative bubbles. It is available for study as a teachable case for anyone considering the next analogous wave, whatever it turns out to be.

Why even good projects can be bad investments

Some crypto projects have legitimate technology and earnest teams. Their tokens can still be poor investments, for reasons that have nothing to do with the technology. The token's price depends on supply schedule, demand from users (versus speculators), liquidity, and market sentiment. A project can deliver everything its developers promised and still see its token decline ninety percent because the supply schedule outpaced adoption.

This is unintuitive for readers who think of crypto investing as betting on which technology will succeed. The technology is one input. The token economics — how supply grows, how demand is generated, how value flows back to holders — are equally important. A project worth using is not always a project worth holding the token of. The honest question is not just "does this project work" but "if this project works, does the token I am buying capture meaningful value from that success?" The two questions have different answers more often than retail buyers realize.

Reading what insiders own

Most token projects publish information about how much of the supply is held by founders, early investors, and insiders, and on what schedule those holdings unlock. The information is often in the project's documentation, sometimes in a separately published transparency report, occasionally only on the blockchain itself. Reading it requires patience but no special skill.

The questions worth asking: How much of the total supply is held by insiders, and how much is in public circulation? When do the largest insider holdings become liquid? Have insiders sold portions of their holdings before, and at what prices? A project where insiders hold most of the supply, with large unlocks coming in the near future, has a structural overhang that almost guarantees selling pressure regardless of what the technology does. The reader who checks the schedule before buying is making a much more informed decision than the reader who buys based on the chart alone.

Why "due diligence" is harder than it sounds

Cryptocurrency promoters often tell prospective buyers to "do their own research" before purchasing. The phrase sounds responsible. In practice, retail buyers usually do not have access to the kind of information that would allow meaningful research. The team's identities are often pseudonymous or unverifiable. The token's reserves and treasury are sometimes on-chain and sometimes not. The smart-contract code may be open source but is rarely audited by independent firms with names the buyer would recognize. The roadmap and partnerships described in marketing are often unverifiable.

What "do your own research" usually means in practice is that the buyer reads the project's own marketing, watches videos by influencers paid to promote the project, and concludes that they have done research. They have not. They have read the marketing in several formats. The honest research that institutional investors do — verified team identities, audited financials, legal opinions on the security status of the token, technical audits by reputable firms — is usually beyond the reach of retail. The phrase "do your own research" is best understood as a way to shift responsibility to the buyer for decisions made on insufficient information.

Why airdrops and free tokens are not actually free

Crypto projects sometimes give away tokens to early users — a practice called an airdrop. The free tokens feel like a windfall. They are also taxable income at fair market value at the time of receipt, and they create a future capital-gains question when sold. Many recipients of airdrops have ended up owing taxes on tokens whose value collapsed before they could be sold, leaving them with a tax bill but no liquid asset to pay it from.

This is a specific case of a more general principle: free things in crypto often have hidden costs. The token with the high yield has a token-printing schedule that dilutes you faster than the yield pays. The free NFT has a transaction fee on every transfer. The promotional reward has tax implications no one mentioned. The reader participating in any crypto promotion should ask, before participating, what the actual full cost looks like. The marketing emphasizes the upside. The honest evaluation includes everything, including the parts the marketing left out.

> *If the only reason to buy a token is that other people are buying it, the only reason it will keep rising is that more people will buy it. That is the definition of a queue, not an investment.*

Chapter 23

Scams and Fraud in Day Trading

The retail trading ecosystem includes legitimate brokers, regulated platforms, honest educators — and a sea of operators whose business is selling the dream of trading rather than producing trading returns. This chapter maps the landscape so the reader can recognize the categories at sight.

Outright fraud

At the most extreme end sit unregistered brokers operating from offshore jurisdictions who accept deposits and refuse withdrawals. "Investment firms" that turn out to be Ponzi schemes. Signal services and copy-trading platforms with fabricated track records. Crypto rug-pulls where the development team disappears with the project's funds. Regulatory agencies in most jurisdictions maintain warning lists of named operators, and search engines can quickly surface complaint patterns.

The simplest defense is regulatory verification. Any U.S. broker should appear in FINRA's BrokerCheck database. Any registered investment advisor should appear in the SEC's IAPD database. Any unregistered operator soliciting accounts is, regardless of the marketing, a high-probability fraud.

Guru economics

A more populated category is the trading-education business. The economics are straightforward and worth understanding. An instructor who can recruit a thousand subscribers at fifty dollars per month generates six hundred thousand dollars per year in revenue from the course business alone. The same instructor's actual trading account, even if successful, is a smaller and less reliable income source. The rational instructor optimizes for the course business. The marketing emphasizes lifestyle imagery, bold claims, and time-limited offers, because those convert subscribers, not because they describe the trading reality.

Some instructors are honest about the structure and provide genuine educational value. Many are not. The signal worth watching is the focus of the marketing and the verifiability of the trading claims. Honest educators show audited track records, separate teaching income from trading income clearly, and decline to make outsized promises. Dishonest ones do the opposite. The reader can usually tell them apart in five minutes of careful reading.

Pump groups

Coordinated pump groups exist in every retail-accessible market. Members commit to buying a designated asset at a coordinated time, with the expectation of selling into retail buyers who arrive after the price moves. The internal arithmetic guarantees that a substantial fraction of group members lose, because the total demand is bounded and the order of buying and selling determines who profits. Outsiders who follow the public signs of a pump are even more reliably the exit liquidity.

Self-defense checklist

- Verify regulatory registration before depositing funds. Use BrokerCheck (FINRA) and IAPD (SEC) for U.S.-based; look up local equivalents elsewhere.
- Ask explicitly how the platform makes money. If the answer is unclear, the answer is "from you, in ways the marketing does not feature."
- Demand audited track records for any subscription that includes trade signals or copy trading. Refuse to subscribe to unaudited claims, regardless of the screenshots.
- Treat "limited-time" pricing on educational products as a high-pressure sales tactic, because that is what it is.
- If you cannot withdraw funds easily, you do not have funds. Test withdrawal early, before depositing meaningful amounts.
- Be especially skeptical of any platform that combines high leverage, offshore registration, and aggressive influencer marketing. The combination is a fraud signature.

How to verify a broker in five minutes

Before depositing money with any broker, the diligence required is small and worth doing every time. In the United States, the FINRA BrokerCheck database lists every registered broker-dealer and individual broker, along with disciplinary history. The SEC's IAPD database does the same for investment advisors. Both are free and take less than five minutes to search.

If the broker is not in the relevant database, that is the answer. The broker is not registered, the regulatory protections do not apply, and the marketing materials are presenting a service that is not what it claims to be. Outside the United States, every major financial regulator maintains an analogous public registry. The five minutes spent confirming registration is the cheapest insurance available against the worst class of trading-related fraud.

The withdrawal test

If you do open an account with a new broker, the most useful early test is to deposit a small amount and then immediately attempt to withdraw it. A legitimate broker processes the withdrawal cleanly, on the disclosed schedule, with no surprises. A fraudulent broker introduces friction: unexpected verification requirements, delays, partial withdrawals, fees that were not disclosed, or outright refusal.

The cost of running this test is essentially zero, and it surfaces the most important risk before any meaningful money is at stake. A reader who feels foolish testing a respected broker is misjudging the asymmetry. The respected broker handles the test in minutes. The bad broker reveals itself before significant losses are possible. There is no downside to checking.

The funded-trader trap

A growing category of retail offerings sells "funded trader" programs. The pitch: pay an evaluation fee, pass a simulated trading challenge, and receive access to a funded account where the firm provides capital and you keep most of the profits. The marketing emphasizes the upside: trade with the firm's money, no personal risk beyond the evaluation fee.

The economics tell a different story. The evaluation fee is the firm's primary revenue. Pass rates are extremely low — typically under five percent — and many traders pay multiple evaluation fees before passing or quitting. Once funded, traders are subject to additional rules and scaling restrictions that disqualify them at small drawdowns. Some firms operate as legitimate talent-discovery operations; many are essentially fee-extraction businesses dressed in professional vocabulary. Diligence on these programs follows the same rules as any other: verify regulatory standing, demand audited payout records, and read the rules carefully before paying anything.

Common red flags in trading marketing

- Lifestyle imagery: rented mansions, leased exotic cars, staged vacations. Real successful traders rarely advertise.
- Limited-time offers and countdown timers. The pressure is the product.
- Testimonials without verifiable identities. Names, photos, and last initials are not enough.
- Specific income claims ("I made $50,000 last month") without audited records.
- Requests to deposit funds with the promoter rather than into your own brokerage account.
- Promises of guaranteed returns or near-zero risk. Both are red flags in any market.
- Unregistered status with regulators. Always verifiable. Always disqualifying.
- Heavy social-media advertising paired with no presence on professional industry forums.
- Pressure to recruit others ("refer a friend and earn"). The structure may be a multi-level marketing scheme dressed as trading.

Why testimonials are nearly worthless

Testimonials in trading marketing carry almost no information. They are selected by the marketer to support the sale. The participants who lost money are not contacted for testimonials, and even if they were, the marketer would not include them. The visible testimonials therefore represent the best-case sample of the most enthusiastic users, not a typical experience.

Even if every testimonial is genuine, they do not tell you what fraction of users had similar outcomes. Did a hundred satisfied customers come from a thousand total users (a ten percent success rate, which is poor) or from a million (a one in ten thousand rate, which is essentially random luck)? The marketing never says. The reader evaluating any retail trading product should treat testimonials as decorative, not evidential, and should ask instead for audited aggregate performance data — which is rarely provided, because it rarely supports the sale.

How to verify any guru in five minutes

Before paying any guru anything, the diligence required is small and worth doing every time. Search the guru's name plus the words "fraud," "complaint," and "refund" — separately for each. Check whether the guru is registered with any relevant regulator. Look at the date the guru's website and social-media accounts were created; recent creation dates combined with claims of long experience are a warning sign. Read the lowest-rated reviews of any course or product, paying attention to specific claims about what was promised versus delivered. Search for the guru's claimed verifiable accomplishments — published work, regulatory filings, professional history — and check whether they actually exist.

This takes about five minutes. It catches the worst frauds before any money changes hands. It also catches a substantial fraction of the in-between cases — people who are not exactly fraudulent but whose claims do not survive five minutes of scrutiny. The reader who runs this check on every prospective guru, every time, is operating with dramatically less risk than the reader who skips it. The guru whose marketing depends on the reader skipping the check is not the guru you want to learn from.

Why the best brokers do not advertise heavily

There is a rough inverse relationship in financial services between how much a firm advertises to retail and how good its actual offerings are. The largest, most established, lowest-cost mutual fund and brokerage firms do some advertising, but their growth over decades has been driven mostly by the strength of their products, the clarity of their fees, and the loyalty of their existing customers. The firms that advertise most aggressively to retail tend to be ones whose products do not stand on their own and require marketing to compete.

This is not a perfect rule. Some good firms advertise heavily, and some poor firms advertise modestly. But it is a useful filter. A reader trying to choose a financial-services provider should pay attention to whether the firm's reputation rests primarily on customer experience or primarily on marketing. The first kind tends to be cheaper, more trustworthy, and better aligned with the customer's interests. The second tends to charge more, push specific products, and treat marketing as a substitute for actual quality.

Why the price of the course is the wrong question

When evaluating a paid trading product, the most common question retail buyers ask is whether the price is reasonable. The honest answer is that the price is the wrong question. A two-thousand-dollar course that teaches nothing useful is expensive at any price. A free course that produces real understanding is valuable even if the time spent is large. The right question is not what the course costs, but what the course actually delivers, evaluated against free alternatives that already exist. Most paid retail trading products fail this comparison. The reader who asks the right question saves themselves the cost of finding out the hard way.

If selling courses about trading is more profitable than trading, the rational instructor sells courses. Read the marketing accordingly.

Chapter 24

Consultation and Signal Services

Two adjacent industries promise to remove the hardest parts of trading — discipline, emotion, time at the screen — by handing the decisions to someone else. The two are paid consultation services and broadcast signal services. Both are sometimes delivered honestly and far more often delivered as marketing. This chapter walks through them plainly.

Paid consultation and one-on-one mentorship

Some traders sell hourly or program-based consulting: structured curricula, video calls, code reviews, account reviews. The honest version of this looks like any other professional service — a clearly priced engagement, deliverables that can be evaluated, references from real clients with verifiable outcomes. The dishonest version is a packaged program with a charismatic salesperson, vague claims about "transformation," and a price that scales with the appearance of premium service rather than with measurable instruction.

Real teachers exist. They charge reasonable fees, point students toward free resources first, and recommend that small traders not trade at all until specific criteria are met. They are findable but require careful diligence.

Signal services

A signal service publishes trade ideas — entries, exits, and stop levels — to subscribers, typically through a private channel. The economics scale: the same signal goes to one subscriber or ten thousand, with marginal cost essentially zero. The structural problems are several:

- Slippage on widely broadcast signals: many subscribers placing the same order in the same window degrades the realized fill for all of them.

- Track-record manipulation: post-hoc edits, cherry-picked screenshots, timing differences between signal posting and subscriber action.
- Selection bias: services with bad runs disappear; services on good runs market aggressively. The visible signal services are not a random sample.
- Misalignment of incentives: signal-service revenue scales with subscribers, not with subscriber outcomes.

There are honest signal services with audited records and legitimate education behind them. They are a minority. The fastest screen is to demand a verifiable, third-party audited track record over multiple years and across multiple market regimes. Anything less is a subscription, not a signal service.

Copy trading

Copy-trading platforms automate the signal-following step: subscribers' accounts mirror the trades of selected lead traders, scaled to the subscriber's account size. The platforms publicize lead-trader returns. The publication is technically accurate and structurally misleading. Lead traders with high returns over short windows are usually those who took the largest risks; the same risks that produced the visible upside also produce the periodic blowups that remove lead traders from the platform. New subscribers see only the survivors.

The platform's revenue grows with the volume of copying activity, which is maximized when subscribers chase recent winners. The structure encourages the worst possible behavior: high turnover among lead-trader allocations, chasing recent performance, abandoning leads after a drawdown. Empirical studies of copy-trading platforms repeatedly find net subscriber returns substantially below buy-and-hold benchmarks, even when individual lead-trader returns look attractive.

How to use these services if you must

- Treat any subscription cost as money that has to be earned back before claiming the service was worth it.
- Apply the same skepticism to advertised win rates as you would to any unsolicited investment offer.
- Test the service in paper trading or with very small size for at least six months before committing real capital.
- Keep your own journal of every signal taken, the realized result, and your honest evaluation of whether the service helped versus hurt.
- Cancel quickly when the answer is clear. Avoid the sunk-cost trap of justifying a year of subscriptions because you have already paid for six months.

What audited means, exactly

When a signal service or trading instructor claims a track record, the question to ask is whether the record is audited and by whom. Audited, in this context, means that an independent third party — a registered accounting firm or a regulated audit organization — has reviewed the trade history, confirmed that the trades were actually placed at the times and prices claimed, and confirmed that the published returns reflect realistic transaction costs.

Audited records are the exception, not the rule, in retail signal services. Most published track records are screenshots, self-reported numbers, or selectively chosen periods. Some are entirely fabricated. A reader considering a paid signal service should refuse to accept anything less than a full audited record across multiple years and multiple market regimes. If the service cannot produce one, the service does not have the kind of track record worth paying for.

Why copying winners often loses

Copy-trading platforms publish lists of "top traders" with high recent returns and offer to mirror their trades automatically. The mechanism sounds straightforward and reliably underperforms expectations. The reasons are well documented in research.

First, the highest-returning traders over short windows are usually the ones taking the largest risks. The same risk that produced the visible upside also produces blowups, and the blowups are how lead traders disappear from the platform. New subscribers see only the survivors, never the casualties. Second, the platform's revenue grows with the volume of copying activity, which is maximized when subscribers chase recent winners. The structure encourages exactly the wrong behavior — high turnover, performance-chasing, abandoning leads at the bottom of drawdowns. Third, simultaneous execution by many subscribers degrades fills and reduces any edge the lead trader might have had. Across all of these factors, empirical studies of copy-trading platforms repeatedly find that net subscriber returns substantially lag simple buy-and-hold benchmarks.

How a serious mentor would actually behave

A genuinely useful trading mentor — and they exist — does several things consistently. They tell prospective students not to trade with money they cannot afford to lose. They recommend free resources first and paid programs only when those have been exhausted. They show audited records or admit they do not have them. They charge transparent fees and do not pressure students with limited-time offers. They acknowledge that most students will not become full-time profitable traders, and they mean it.

If you have found such a mentor, you have found a rare thing. Pay them their reasonable fee and learn what they have to teach. If you have found someone whose marketing emphasizes their lifestyle, whose track record is unverifiable, whose program is sold with countdown timers and limited-time pricing, you have found a salesperson. The salesperson may be sincere about wanting to help, but they are still a salesperson, and the sale is structured to benefit them more than you.

What the math of subscriptions does to teaching

When a teacher's main income comes from subscriptions, the economic incentive favors keeping subscribers paying for as long as possible. Students who become genuinely independent — who learn enough that they no longer need the subscription — represent lost revenue. The structure does not require the teacher to be cynical, but it does shape what gets taught.

The honest version of trading education would help students reach independence quickly, recommend free resources where they exist, and tell most students that they should not trade with money they cannot afford to lose. The subscription version tends to teach systems just complex enough that students keep returning for help. Both kinds of teachers exist. The reader trying to choose between them should look at how quickly the teacher is willing to make themselves obsolete to a successful student. The honest ones are willing. The subscription-driven ones are not.

What a successful student actually looks like

Almost every retail trading instructor publishes occasional examples of successful students. The students appear young, articulate, and visibly enthusiastic. They describe how the program changed their lives. The marketing presents them as representative outcomes.

If you wanted to know the truth about a program's outcomes, you would need to talk to the students who quit, who lost money, or who concluded that the program did not help them. They are not on the marketing page. They are not in the live events. They have moved on with lives that no longer involve the program. Their absence from the visible record is not an accident. It is how the marketing works. A reader trying to evaluate a program honestly should assume that the visible students are the best one or two percent of the total, and that the typical student has a much more ordinary outcome — at best.

What free resources can actually teach you

Before paying anyone for trading or investing education, an honest reader should exhaust the substantial body of free resources that already exists. The Berkshire Hathaway shareholder letters are free and contain decades of investing wisdom. Many academic papers on retail trading are open-access. The SEC and FINRA publish extensive plain-language investor education for free. Books from major libraries cover almost every topic any paid course would teach.

A reader who spends fifty hours with these free resources before paying anything for paid education is in a much better position to evaluate paid offerings. They know what the actual concepts are. They have seen what good explanation looks like. They can recognize when a paid course is recycling free material with extra marketing. The exhaustion of free resources is the first defense against paying for things that do not need to be paid for. Most retail readers skip this step. The ones who do not save substantial money and learn substantially more.

What a real teacher's incentives look like

A real teacher of any subject — including trading — has incentives that align with student success. They want students to learn enough to no longer need the teacher. They want students to recommend the teacher to others, which requires those students to have actually benefited. They are willing to be evaluated on outcomes, including ones that took years to materialize. They charge in proportion to what they actually deliver, not in proportion to what marketing can convince students they are getting.

Trading instructors with these incentives exist. They are often hard to find because they do not advertise heavily, do not run high-pressure sales funnels, and do not promise quick results. The reader looking for a real teacher should be willing to spend time finding one, and should treat any instructor whose marketing relies on aggressive sales tactics as a warning sign rather than a feature. The teacher whose incentives are aligned with your success looks different from the teacher whose incentives are aligned with closing the sale this week. The difference is visible if you know what to look for.

Chapter 25

Trading Bots and Auto Trading

Trading bots and auto-trading platforms promise the same thing as signal services, plus one more thing: removal of the human entirely. The pitch is appealing. No emotion, no fatigue, no missed signals. The reality usually does not deliver.

What a bot actually is

A trading bot is a program that executes trades from a defined rule set. The rules can be simple ("if RSI is below 30, buy; sell when RSI is above 70") or arbitrarily complex. The rules can be the user's own or can be supplied by the bot vendor. Some platforms let users build rules visually; others sell ready-made strategies.

Bots are not magic. They are just software that places trades on a schedule. Whether they make money depends entirely on whether the rules they execute have a real edge after costs, and whether that edge persists out of sample. Most bot rules sold to retail do not.

Backtests are not real performance

The standard sales pitch for a retail bot is a backtest showing impressive returns over historical data. There are several things the marketing does not emphasize. First, almost any rule with enough adjustable parameters can be tuned to fit past data perfectly; the same rule on new data typically performs much worse. Second, backtests typically assume zero spread, zero slippage, and instant fills, none of which are realistic. Third, the markets the bot was tested on may behave very differently in the next regime.

When a vendor will not show live performance — only backtests — the absence is informative. When the vendor will show live performance but only over a short window or only on a small live account, that is informative too.

Why a real edge is usually not for sale

If a bot genuinely produced consistent, risk-adjusted returns net of costs, the rational owner of the rules would deploy the rules with their own capital and keep the profits. Selling the rules dilutes the edge (more participants compete for the same opportunities) and caps the income (subscription revenue is bounded). The fact that a strategy is sold as a subscription, rather than being deployed as a hedge fund, is itself information about its likely quality.

A small minority of vendors are honest exceptions: they sell tooling that helps traders implement their own rules better, rather than selling the rules themselves. Tooling can be useful. Bots that promise specific returns by following specific signals usually cannot back the promise up.

AI and the new generation

Recent products use the language of artificial intelligence and machine learning. Some genuinely incorporate modern statistical methods. Many simply use the vocabulary as marketing. The same diligence questions apply. Demand audited live performance over multiple regimes. Refuse to be impressed by backtests. Notice when the marketing emphasizes the technology rather than the realized results. AI is a real and powerful set of tools. It is also an exceptionally effective marketing wrapper for products that do not work.

Practical guidance

- If you want to automate your own rules, learn enough programming to do it yourself. The control and transparency are worth the effort.
- Be especially suspicious of any bot that requires its custody of your funds rather than running through your

existing brokerage account.

- Test any automated strategy on paper or with very small size for months before scaling up.
- Build in hard kill switches: maximum daily loss, maximum drawdown from peak, maximum position size. Bots can run away in unusual market conditions, and a kill switch is the difference between a bad day and a closed account.
- Recognize that automating a losing strategy turns a slow loss into a fast one. Edge first, then automation.

Why backtests lie politely

A backtest is a simulation of how a trading rule would have performed on historical data. It is the standard sales tool for a retail trading bot, and it is one of the easier things to fake without technically lying. The most common failure modes:

- Curve-fitting: the rule has so many adjustable parameters that it can be tuned to fit any past data perfectly. The same rule on new data performs no better than coin flips.
- Survivorship bias: the rule is tested on stocks or coins that exist today, ignoring the ones that went bankrupt or were delisted along the way.
- Look-ahead bias: the rule uses information that, in real time, would not have been available at the moment the trade was placed.
- Unrealistic costs: the simulation assumes zero spread, zero slippage, and instant fills, none of which are realistic for retail traders.
- Cherry-picked windows: the displayed track record covers a period that happened to favor the strategy, while quietly ignoring periods where it did not.

An honestly run backtest, with realistic costs and out-of-sample data, almost always shows worse results than a marketing backtest. When a vendor refuses to share methodology details, refuses to test on out-of-sample data, or refuses to show live performance, the absence is informative.

The asymmetry that explains why bots are sold

Suppose, for the sake of argument, that you have built a trading bot that produces consistent risk-adjusted returns net of costs. What would the rational owner of that bot do? Almost certainly, deploy it with their own capital, scale up as the strategy proves itself, and keep the profits. Selling subscriptions to use the bot dilutes the edge — every additional user competes for the same opportunities — and caps the income at whatever subscribers will pay.

The fact that a bot is sold as a subscription, rather than being deployed by its creator, is itself information about its likely quality. There are honest exceptions: vendors who sell tooling that helps users implement their own rules, rather than selling specific rules. The tooling can be useful. Bots that promise specific returns by following specific signals usually cannot back the promise up. The honest test is to ask: if this works as well as the marketing says, why is the creator selling it instead of using it?

If you want to automate, build it yourself

If you genuinely want to automate part of your trading, the most defensible path is to learn enough programming to build the automation yourself. The skills are not as specialized as they look. A reader with no prior coding experience can, within a few months of focused effort, learn enough Python to read brokerage data, execute simple rules, and analyze results.

The benefit is not just cost savings. It is transparency. You know exactly what your code does, because you wrote it. You know what data it uses. You know what assumptions it makes. None of that is true of a bot purchased as a subscription, which is generally a black box. The investment of learning is real, and not everyone wants to make it. For those who do, the result is a small set of tools that does exactly what the trader wanted, with no hidden subscription costs and no vendor risk.

When a kill switch becomes essential

Any automated trading system needs a kill switch — a set of conditions under which the system stops trading automatically, regardless of what the rules would otherwise do. Standard kill conditions include maximum daily loss in dollars, maximum drawdown from peak equity, maximum number of consecutive losing trades, and maximum total positions open at one time.

The kill switch matters because automated systems can fail in ways human traders would not. A bug can place orders much larger than intended. A market data feed can lag, causing the system to trade on stale prices. A market event can produce a sequence of losses far larger than any historical scenario the system was tested against. Without a kill switch, the system keeps trading through any of these scenarios. With one, the worst outcome is bounded. Building the kill switch is the first thing the developer of any automated system should do, before optimizing the trading rules. Many retail bot users skip it entirely. Those are the ones who eventually wake up to a destroyed account.

Why simple beats clever in software

Software engineers have a saying: complexity is the enemy. The same is true in automated trading. A simple system with three or four well-tested rules tends to be more robust than a complex one with dozens of conditional behaviors. Each additional rule adds opportunities for bugs, for unexpected interactions, for behavior the developer did not anticipate. In real markets, with real money on the line, those unexpected behaviors are exactly the failures that wipe accounts.

The retail trading bot industry tends to sell the opposite — complex systems with many rules, advanced indicators, and elaborate optimization. The complexity is partly real (some systems do work better with more rules) and partly marketing (complexity makes the system feel sophisticated, justifying the price). The honest version of automated trading favors simple, well-understood rules, kill switches that protect against unexpected behavior, and constant monitoring during the early months of live deployment. The clever version usually breaks in ways the developer did not see coming.

Why most automated systems eventually break

Even well-designed automated trading systems eventually break. Markets change in ways the system was not tested against. A new regulatory rule changes how a venue operates. A data feed adds a delay that interacts badly with the system's assumptions. A market event moves prices faster than the system can react. Each of these is rare in any given week, common across years of operation.

The breakage is the point at which the trader's monitoring matters most. A system that is monitored daily catches most failures within a few hours. A system that is left to run unattended for weeks can produce losses far larger than any reasonable design would have permitted. The trader who automates trading and then disengages from the system has not actually automated trading; they have abandoned it to a process that will eventually fail. Automation reduces the trader's moment-to-moment work. It does not eliminate the work entirely. The work that remains is supervisory.

What buying a bot actually buys you

When a retail trader buys access to a trading bot, they usually receive: the right to use the software for a defined period, a set of trading rules they cannot fully inspect, customer support of varying quality, and an ongoing subscription cost. They do not receive: an audited live track record, the right to inspect the source code, the source code's history of changes, or any guarantee that the rules will keep working in the future.

The transaction is, in effect, paying a subscription for software whose actual quality cannot be verified. The vendor has no incentive to share the information that would allow verification, because verification would expose the bot's real performance, which is usually worse than the marketing suggests. The reader buying a bot is buying a black box and trusting that the box does what the marketing says. Most boxes do not. The honest path, for readers who want automated trading, is to learn enough to build their own simple system, where they can see exactly what it does and adjust it when needed.

If a system genuinely worked, the system would not be for sale. It would be deployed.

Chapter 26

Lack of Stability and Financial Future

Conventional employment, with all its frustrations, provides stability features that day trading simply does not. This chapter is not a defense of every job. It is an honest accounting of what a job provides, what self-directed day trading does not, and what the absence of those features means over a working lifetime.

Income stability

A salaried worker earns a predictable amount each month. The amount may be inadequate or unfairly low, but it is predictable. Day trading income, even for the rare profitable trader, is not. Profitable months alternate with break-even and losing ones, and the variance of monthly income is typically high enough to make household budgeting materially harder. Lenders do not extend credit on the basis of trading income without a long, audited track record. Mortgage applications, car loans, and personal credit lines all become more difficult.

Benefits

Employer-sponsored health insurance, retirement matching, life and disability insurance, paid time off, and parental leave have material monetary value that salary alone understates. A self-directed trader replicates these benefits at higher cost or, more commonly, goes without. The risk profile of going without health insurance or disability coverage is asymmetric — most years it costs nothing, occasional years it costs everything.

Retirement contributions

Employer retirement plans, employer matches, and the automatic discipline of payroll-deduction contributions produce a pattern of long-term saving that, compounded across a career, dwarfs the realized returns of most active trading. A worker contributing fifteen percent of a moderate salary, half matched by an employer, into a low-cost target-date fund will accumulate a meaningful retirement balance over a thirty-five-year career, without making a single trading decision. The same worker who skips that contribution to fund a trading account, even one that produces small positive returns, almost never reaches the same endpoint.

Career capital

Years of full-time employment build skills, credentials, and a professional network. None of these are visible on any single day. All of them are valuable across decades. A trader who steps out of the workforce for several years to trade full-time pays an opportunity cost not just in foregone salary but in foregone career trajectory: the promotion not earned, the manager experience not built, the network not extended. Returning to traditional employment after a multi-year trading break is harder than the trader anticipated when they made the original choice.

Identity and structure

Work provides daily structure, social contact, and a sense of purpose that humans, on average, find healthy. Removing those scaffolds, especially while substituting an isolating and stressful self-directed activity, has consequences for mental health, social life, and long-run satisfaction that previous chapters have already covered.

What the data say about "trading for income"

Studies across multiple jurisdictions converge on a similar finding. Only a small minority of retail day traders earn enough, after costs, to substitute for ordinary employment income. A widely cited Brazilian study found that of those who persisted in day trading for more than three hundred sessions, only about three percent earned more than the country's minimum wage, and roughly one percent earned more than a bank teller. Studies of Taiwanese and Korean traders find similar concentrations of net positive returns in the upper single-digit percentage of long-term participants. The large majority lose money over multi-year horizons.

The realistic alternative

The argument for stability does not require accepting any particular job, any particular career, or any particular lifestyle. It requires recognizing that the structural features of a stable income source — predictable cash flow, benefits, retirement contributions, career compounding — are valuable, and that day trading does not produce them for the typical participant. Many sources of income are compatible with these features. Salaried employment is one. Self-employment with regular invoicing is another. Building a real business with paying customers is a third. Day trading, on the data, is none of them.

What employer benefits actually add up to

When people compare salaries, they usually compare gross pay. The fuller comparison includes the benefits that come with most employment and that a self-employed trader has to replace at their own cost or skip. A typical employer-sponsored health insurance plan, paid largely by the employer, can be worth fifteen to twenty thousand dollars a year for a family. Employer matching of retirement contributions, where it exists, often adds another three to six percent of salary as free money. Paid time off, sick days, parental leave, and disability insurance each have real dollar value.

A trader replacing all of these out of pocket is paying tens of thousands of dollars per year for what employment used to provide automatically. A trader skipping them is gambling against the asymmetric risk that something will go wrong — illness, injury, a child's surprise medical event — that the absent insurance would have covered.

The trap of starting a year late

Compounding rewards starting early and punishes delay in non-obvious ways. A worker who starts contributing five hundred dollars a month to a retirement account at age twenty-five, and never increases the amount, accumulates a sizable balance by sixty-five — often well into seven figures, depending on assumed returns. The same worker starting at thirty-five, ten years later, ends with a noticeably smaller balance for the same contributions, because the missing decade is the decade where compounding had the longest runway.

Time spent attempting to day trade for a living, while not contributing to a retirement account, is time the missed contributions cannot be recovered. The trader who tries day trading for five years, breaks even, and returns to traditional employment has lost more than zero — they have lost five years of compounding on contributions that were never made. The cost is invisible at the time and very visible at the far end of a working life.

Career capital is also compounding

Skills, credentials, and professional networks are not glamorous, but they compound much like money. Five years of full-time work in a field, done well, build technical skills, accumulate trust with colleagues, and create the network that surfaces the next opportunity. Five years of full-time day trading, even if the trader breaks even on the trading itself, build none of those things. The trader returning to traditional employment after a multi-year break has to rebuild what they would have accumulated naturally if they had stayed.

This is one of the reasons that experienced traders who quit usually advise newcomers not to quit their day jobs. The day job is not just a hedge against trading losses. It is the structure that builds career capital across decades, in a way that pure trading does not. The decision to leave it is bigger than it usually feels in the moment of leaving.

What the data say across countries

Studies in different countries reach roughly the same conclusion. A widely cited study of Brazilian futures traders found that of those who persisted in day trading for more than three hundred sessions, only about three percent earned more than the country's minimum wage, and roughly one percent earned more than a bank teller. Studies of Korean and Taiwanese retail traders have found similarly stark concentration of net positive returns in the upper single-digit percentage of long-term participants.

These are not edge-case studies. They cover hundreds of thousands of traders across decades, in markets with the same kind of access ordinary retail traders have. The conclusion is consistent across markets and time periods: the activity does not, on the data, work as a way to replace ordinary employment income for the vast majority of people who attempt it.

What sequence of returns risk means

A specific financial risk that affects long-term investors, especially around retirement, is sequence of returns risk. The same average return can produce very different outcomes depending on the order in which good and bad years arrive. A retiree who experiences a major drawdown early in retirement, while withdrawing money for living expenses, can run out of funds decades earlier than a retiree with the same average return whose drawdown happens late.

The math is unforgiving. Drawing from a depleted base in early years removes the capital that would have compounded through the subsequent recovery. This is the strongest argument for de-risking portfolios as retirement approaches and for maintaining cash buffers that allow retirees to avoid forced selling during early-retirement bear markets. Day trading income, which is itself volatile, multiplies sequence risk rather than mitigating it. A household relying on volatile income through years near retirement is taking a risk most professional planners would advise against.

Why the gap between visible and invisible exits matters

The trader who succeeded for ten years and bought a house with their winnings is visible. They write articles. They appear on podcasts. They sell courses. The trader who tried for ten years, lost half their savings, and quietly returned to traditional employment is not visible. They do not write articles. They are not interviewed. The picture of who succeeds at full-time trading, drawn from public information alone, is biased toward the visible exits and silent about the rest.

When evaluating whether to attempt full-time trading, the relevant question is the full distribution of outcomes for people who tried, weighted by how often each outcome occurred. The visible tail is a small share of that distribution. The bulk is in the silent middle and lower regions. A reader contemplating the attempt should reason about the bulk, not the tail.

Why career re-entry is harder than people expect

A trader who tries full-time trading for several years and concludes that they want to return to traditional employment often finds the re-entry harder than they expected. The resume gap is visible. Recruiters are skeptical. The skills that were current when the trader left have moved on. The professional network that would have surfaced opportunities has thinned. The trader who took five years off to trade may find that the salary they re-enter at is meaningfully lower than the one they left.

This is not always the case. Some industries are forgiving of gaps. Some employers value the discipline that consistent self-directed activity demonstrates, even if it did not produce the financial outcomes the trader hoped for. But the structural friction is real, and the reader contemplating a full-time trading attempt should price it into the decision. The opportunity cost is not just the lost salary during the trading years. It is also the reduced earning potential after, if the attempt does not work out and traditional employment becomes the next chapter.

What the typical successful exit looks like

The traders who exit successfully — meaning they stop trading and walk away with more than they started with — usually share a few features. They had other income while trading, so the trading was never required to pay the bills. They sized small enough that any single drawdown was survivable. They kept the trading capital walled off from real savings. They quit when they noticed that their realized returns over years did not justify the time and stress, and they did not try to recover everything before quitting. They returned to or continued in conventional careers without much fanfare.

These exits do not produce content. They are quiet, undramatic, often uncelebrated. The trader simply concludes that the activity is not worth it and stops. This is the most common positive exit pattern, and it is invisible in the public conversation about trading because it is uninteresting to anyone who is not the trader. The dramatic exit — the one with the screenshot of the big win and the new car — is what gets attention. The quiet exit, where the trader simply moves on, is the one most people who try trading should aim for if they cannot match the unrealistic visible alternative.

Why retirement timing is mostly out of your control

Many people imagine retirement as a moment they will choose. The honest pattern is different. Retirements happen for many reasons, and most of them are not entirely the retiree's choice. Health changes. A spouse's health changes. A layoff arrives unexpectedly in late career. A parent needs care. The job changes in ways that make staying difficult. The financial plan that assumes retirement will start exactly at sixty-five, with full earning years preserved up to that point, is making an assumption that often does not hold.

The defense is to plan as if retirement might begin earlier than expected. Save more aggressively in the highest-earning years. Build the retirement balance to the point where stopping work at sixty would be acceptable, even if you intend to work past that. The household with this margin handles unexpected timing without crisis. The household without it discovers, when the unexpected happens, that their plans were based on conditions they could not actually guarantee. The earlier the contingency is built in, the cheaper it is to build.

> *Career capital compounds quietly and reliably. Trading capital compounds loudly when it works and disappears loudly when it does not.*

Chapter 27

Better and Safer Alternatives

If day trading is, on the data, a poor route to building wealth for the typical participant, what is a better route? This chapter outlines the alternative concretely. None of it is original. All of it is well supported by both academic research and the lived experience of investors who quietly built durable wealth without staring at one-minute candles.

The diversified, low-cost index portfolio

The single highest-probability strategy for most readers is a portfolio of low-cost broad-market index funds, held across asset classes appropriate to the reader's time horizon and risk tolerance. The U.S. Securities and Exchange Commission's investor-education materials emphasize diversification — across asset classes, geographies, and individual securities — as a core risk-reducer that does not require predicting the future.

A simple implementation might be:

- A broad U.S. equity index fund (total stock market or S&P 500), expense ratio under 0.10 percent.
- A broad international equity index fund (developed and emerging markets), expense ratio under 0.20 percent.
- A broad U.S. bond index fund, expense ratio under 0.10 percent.
- Optionally, a small allocation to inflation-protected bonds for inflation insurance.
- Optionally, a small allocation to alternatives, sized so a total loss is irrelevant.

The proportions depend on age, time horizon, risk tolerance, and country-specific tax considerations. A young investor with decades of horizon can hold a heavier equity weight; an investor approaching withdrawal needs more bonds. A target-date fund is a sensible single-fund version of this approach, and it adjusts the allocation automatically over time.

Automate contributions

The behavioral edge of the index strategy is amplified by automation. Set up automatic contributions on payday — into an employer retirement plan, an individual retirement account, or a taxable brokerage account — at a rate the household can sustain. The contributions buy more shares when prices are low and fewer when prices are high, mechanically, without the investor having to time anything. Across decades, automatic contributions to broad-market index funds have produced more wealth, more reliably, than virtually any active strategy a typical retail participant could implement.

Order of operations

For most readers in the U.S., the order of operations is:

1. Capture any employer retirement plan match. This is free money and the highest-return action available.
2. Pay off high-interest debt. Carrying credit-card debt at twenty percent annual interest while investing at expected returns of seven to ten percent is mathematically poor.
3. Build an emergency fund of three to six months of essential expenses, in a high-yield savings or money-market account.
4. Maximize tax-advantaged retirement contributions, including IRAs, 401(k)s, and HSAs if eligible.
5. Invest additional savings in a taxable brokerage account, in the same low-cost diversified funds.

Other countries have analogous structures. The principle is universal: tax-advantaged compounding is a structural edge that long-term investors can capture and short-term traders cannot.

What Graham and Buffett actually advise

Benjamin Graham, in *The Intelligent Investor*, draws a careful distinction between two types of investors: the defensive investor, who wants acceptable returns with minimal time and effort, and the enterprising investor, willing to do the work for potentially better outcomes. Graham's central practical recommendation for the defensive investor — that is, for most readers — is a diversified portfolio of stocks and bonds, regularly contributed to and held through cycles. He did not have low-cost index funds in 1949. We do, and they are the cleanest modern implementation of his advice.

Warren Buffett, who learned from Graham, has spent decades repeating the same recommendation in his Berkshire Hathaway shareholder letters. For the typical investor, he writes, the highest-probability path to durable wealth is to consistently contribute to a low-cost broad-market index fund and leave it alone. He has stated publicly that this is the instruction he has left for the cash bequeathed to his own family. The recommendation is free, repeated for decades, and verifiable in the public letter archive.

Both teachers stress the same supporting ideas: use only money you can leave invested for years; keep speculation, if you must speculate, in a small separate account; and remember that the opponent who matters most is the version of yourself that panics in bear markets and feels invincible in bull ones.

Real estate, human capital, insurance

For readers with stable employment and long horizons, owning a primary residence at a price the household can comfortably afford is a reasonable component of long-term wealth-building. The combination of forced equity through mortgage payments and long-run home-price appreciation has produced a non-trivial wealth source for most homeowners over decades. It is not a trade. It is a long-duration commitment with tax advantages and behavioral advantages.

The most underrated investment for most readers, especially younger ones, is in their own earning capacity: education, professional skills, certifications, the network that comes with sustained engagement in a profession. The expected return on a year spent improving genuinely valuable skills, for a typical knowledge worker, is far higher than the expected return on the same hours spent day trading.

Insurance is the foundation that allows the rest of the plan to compound. Health insurance, term life insurance if you have dependents, long-term disability, umbrella liability for households with material assets. The premiums feel like dead money in the years no claim arises. That is what insurance is supposed to feel like. The plan that compounds reliably is the one that survives the rare catastrophic event.

What the boring path looks like in numbers

An investor contributing five hundred dollars per month, starting at age twenty-five, into a diversified portfolio earning a long-run average return in line with historical broad-market data, accumulates a meaningful retirement balance by sixty-five — often well into seven figures, depending on assumed return and contribution growth. The same investor starting at thirty-five reaches a noticeably smaller endpoint. Starting at forty-five, smaller still. Time is the active ingredient. The investor's decisions matter much less than the simple act of starting and continuing.

A simple plan, in plain words

- Spend less than you earn.
- Hold an emergency fund.
- Pay off high-interest debt.
- Invest the rest steadily into diversified, low-cost index funds inside tax-advantaged accounts where possible.
- Insure against catastrophes.
- Look at the account once or twice a year. Do not panic in bear markets. Do not chase in bull markets.
- Keep your career strong. Keep your relationships strong. Keep your health strong. Money is a means, not the end.

This is unglamorous and dramatically more likely to produce financial security than any speculative alternative the same household could pursue. It is also much more likely to leave you with a life you actually enjoy along the way.

What an emergency fund actually does

Before any investing, an emergency fund — three to six months of essential household expenses, held in a high-yield savings account or a money-market fund — is the foundation that makes every other financial decision possible. It absorbs unexpected costs (a car repair, a medical bill, a job change) without forcing the household to sell investments at bad moments. It removes the psychological pressure that drives short-term thinking elsewhere in the financial life.

An emergency fund is not exciting. It does not earn high returns. The point of it is not to earn returns. The point is to be there when something goes wrong, so that the things designed to earn returns can be left alone to do their job. A family with an emergency fund tends to make calmer financial decisions across the board, because they are not constantly one expense away from a crisis.

The order of operations

For most readers in the United States, the order of financial operations that produces the best long-run outcome is reasonably standardized. The pattern is similar in most developed countries, with local variations:

1. Capture any employer retirement plan match. This is free money and the highest-return action available to almost anyone.
2. Pay off high-interest debt. Carrying a credit-card balance at twenty percent annual interest while investing at expected returns of seven to ten percent is mathematically backwards.
3. Build an emergency fund of three to six months of essential expenses, in a high-yield savings or money-market account.
4. Maximize tax-advantaged retirement contributions: IRA, 401(k), and a health savings account if eligible.

5. Invest additional savings in a taxable brokerage account, in the same low-cost diversified funds.

Each step builds on the previous one. Skipping any of them weakens the rest. A reader who follows the steps in order, even at modest amounts, will be in a substantially stronger position five years from now than a reader who tries to skip ahead to investing while still carrying high-interest debt or no emergency fund.

Picking the actual fund

The exact fund choice matters less than picking something diversified and low-cost and contributing regularly. Several large fund families offer broad-market index funds with expense ratios under 0.10 percent. The names will look familiar to anyone who has spent five minutes looking at retirement plans. Vanguard, Fidelity, Schwab, BlackRock's iShares — each offers competent options.

A simple three-fund portfolio holds a U.S. broad-market index fund, an international broad-market index fund, and a U.S. broad-market bond index fund, in proportions appropriate to the investor's age and risk tolerance. A target-date fund — a single fund that adjusts the allocation automatically as the target retirement year approaches — is a sensible single-fund version of the same idea. Either approach is dramatically more likely to produce good long-run outcomes than active management or stock picking, for almost everyone who is not a full-time professional.

What rebalancing actually means

Over time, the proportions of a portfolio drift. After a strong year for stocks, the portfolio holds more stocks than the original target. After a strong year for bonds, the opposite. Rebalancing is the act of selling some of what has done well and buying some of what has lagged, to bring the portfolio back to the target proportions.

Done once a year, or whenever the drift exceeds a defined threshold, rebalancing has two benefits. It mechanically enforces the discipline of selling high and buying low. And it controls risk by preventing the portfolio from drifting into a much riskier or much safer profile than the investor intended. Most modern target-date funds rebalance automatically. Investors managing their own portfolios can do it on a fixed calendar — once a year is fine — and stop checking otherwise.

The role of human capital

For younger readers especially, the most underrated investment is in your own earning capacity. The expected return on a year spent improving genuinely valuable skills, for a typical knowledge worker, is far higher than the expected return on the same hours spent day trading. The compounding works through promotions, equity grants, and access to higher-paying opportunities, all of which then feed the index portfolio.

Education, professional certifications, language skills, the network that comes with sustained engagement in a profession — each of these has a real expected return that beats most short-term financial activities. The reader who invests in human capital first, and in financial capital second, usually ends up with both. The reader who tries to build financial capital while neglecting human capital often ends up with neither.

What a finished plan looks like

A complete personal financial plan does not require sophistication. The version that works for most readers fits on a single page:

- Stable income from work, with employer-sponsored health insurance and retirement match captured.
- High-interest debt eliminated.

- Emergency fund of three to six months of essential expenses, held in cash equivalents.
- Automated monthly contributions into tax-advantaged retirement accounts, invested in diversified low-cost index funds appropriate to age and risk tolerance.
- Additional savings flowing into a taxable brokerage account in the same kinds of funds.
- Adequate insurance: health, term life if you have dependents, long-term disability, and umbrella liability for households with material assets.
- A primary residence, if affordable on a sustainable mortgage, owned long-term.
- Periodic rebalancing — once a year is fine — and otherwise no active management.
- Regular conversation about money with the household, so that decisions are joint and surprises are rare.

This is unglamorous and produces, across decades, financial outcomes that almost no active retail trading approach can match. The mathematics, the empirical research, and the lived experience of millions of patient investors all point in the same direction. The hard part is not knowing what to do. The hard part is doing it consistently, year after year, while the financial media and the social-media feeds are screaming about something that sounds more exciting.

Insurance is the foundation

Long-term financial planning is more vulnerable to catastrophic events than to suboptimal returns. A serious illness without adequate insurance can wipe out a decade of savings. A long-term disability without coverage can end a career mid-curve. A premature death without life insurance can devastate dependents. Insurance — health, disability, term life if you have dependents, umbrella liability for households with meaningful assets — is the foundation that allows the rest of the plan to compound.

The premiums feel like dead money in years no claim arises. That is exactly what insurance is supposed to feel like. The plan that compounds reliably over decades is the one that survives the rare catastrophic event when it eventually occurs. The plan that skipped insurance to invest the premiums in something more exciting often does not survive.

What rebalancing accomplishes

Periodic rebalancing — selling some of what has grown beyond its target weight and buying some of what has lagged — accomplishes two things at once. It keeps the portfolio's risk profile aligned with the investor's plan, preventing drift into a much riskier or much safer mix than intended. And it mechanically enforces a buy-low, sell-high discipline that human emotion cannot enforce on its own.

Done annually, or whenever drift exceeds a defined threshold, rebalancing adds a small but real expected return without requiring market timing. Modern target-date funds rebalance automatically. Investors managing their own portfolios can do it on a fixed calendar — once a year is fine. The discipline matters more than the frequency. A simple rule, followed consistently, produces better outcomes than an elaborate rule followed inconsistently.

The single most important habit

If a reader finishes this book, takes only one action, and changes nothing else, the most valuable single action is automating monthly contributions to a low-cost broad-market index fund inside a tax-advantaged account. That single habit, sustained over decades, produces financial outcomes that almost no active alternative reliably matches. It does not require sophistication. It does not require attention. It does not require avoiding mistakes. It works because time and consistency are doing the work, and the investor's main job is to stay out of the way.

The amount matters less than the consistency. A small automatic contribution, sustained for thirty years, beats a larger contribution that gets started, paused, redirected, and started again. The boring path's strength is that, once set up, it runs without effort. The exciting alternatives all require effort, and the effort eventually flags. The boring path does not need motivation. It is on autopilot, doing what it does every payday, while the rest of life happens.

Why the simple plan is hard

The plan recommended in this chapter is mathematically simple. The hard part is not the math. The hard part is sustaining it through years of financial-media noise telling you that something more exciting is available. Every year, several investment trends will look like obvious winners while you are sitting in a boring index fund. Every year, several friends or relatives will tell you about something they made a lot of money on quickly. Every year, social media will fill with people claiming to have figured out a better way.

Most of the trends fail. Most of the friends did not actually make as much as they claim. Most of the social-media accounts do not have the track record they project. But you cannot prove this in real time, and the temptation to abandon the boring plan is constant. The investor who stays the course does so not because they are smarter than the people chasing trends, but because they have decided in advance to ignore the noise. The decision is made once, in calm, and then defended for decades. That is the real skill of patient investing. It does not look like a skill. It looks like doing nothing while interesting things happen elsewhere. Doing nothing, on this scale, is one of the hardest things a person can do with money.

What to do if you have already lost

Some readers come to this chapter after substantial trading losses are already in the past. The temptation is to feel that the patient path is no longer available, that the lost capital is unrecoverable, that the years are wasted. The temptation is wrong. The patient path is available from any starting point. The recovery may take longer than starting earlier would have, but it begins the moment the new approach starts.

A reader who has lost significant capital trading still has the most important asset intact: their future earning years and the compounding those years can produce. Resume contributing to a low-cost diversified portfolio with whatever you can afford. Resume protecting your career, your relationships, your health. The future is still long. Compounding still works, even on smaller starting balances. The years ahead, used well, are far more valuable than the years behind, regardless of what happened in them. The patient path does not punish past mistakes. It welcomes anyone willing to take it from here forward.

What target-date funds quietly do for you

Target-date funds are a single fund that adjusts the underlying mix of stocks and bonds automatically as the target retirement year approaches. A reader who picks a target-date fund close to their expected retirement year and contributes regularly is delegating most of the asset-allocation decision to the fund. The fund holds a heavy stock allocation when the target is decades away and gradually shifts toward bonds as the target nears.

These funds are not perfect. Their fees are often slightly higher than the cheapest individual index funds, and the glide path may not match every investor's preferences. But for a reader who would otherwise pick allocations based on intuition, change them in response to news, or fail to rebalance entirely, the target-date fund usually produces a better outcome than the do-it-yourself version. The single-decision simplicity is the feature. The reader does not have to remember to rebalance, does not have to decide when to shift toward bonds, does not have to worry about whether the international allocation is right. The fund handles all of it. For most retail investors, this is the right level of involvement: sufficient to capture the benefits of diversified investing, minimal enough not to invite the behavioral mistakes that come from frequent decisions.

What a real fee-only advisor can do

Most readers do not need an advisor for the basic strategy outlined in this chapter. The steps are straightforward enough to follow without paid help. Some readers, however, have situations complex enough that a fee-only fiduciary advisor is worth paying for. These include households with substantial concentrated stock from employment, blended-family estate-planning needs, complicated tax situations, large inheritances arriving on uncertain timelines, or wealth large enough that asset-protection planning becomes worth doing carefully.

The right advisor for these situations charges a flat fee or hourly rate, not a percentage of assets, and is registered as a fiduciary, meaning they are legally required to act in your interest. They do not earn commissions on products they recommend. They will tell you when their advice is general enough that you do not need them. A reader paying any other kind of advisor — one paid by commissions, one not registered as a fiduciary, one whose income depends on selling specific products — is paying for advice whose incentive structure runs against the reader's interest. The fee-only fiduciary version is more expensive in dollars and cheaper in actual cost.

Why the cheapest funds are usually fine

When choosing between similar funds, the question of which one is best can produce hours of analysis. The honest answer for most retail investors is that the cheapest large index fund tracking the relevant index is fine. The differences between the major providers are smaller than the differences in expense ratios, and the expense ratios are tiny. A fund charging 0.03 percent and a fund charging 0.05 percent will produce essentially identical results over decades, and either one will dramatically outperform an actively managed fund charging one percent.

The hours spent agonizing over which large-cap U.S. equity index fund is best could be more usefully spent on increasing the savings rate, paying down high-interest debt, or building the emergency fund. The fund choice is the easy part. The hard part is the discipline of contributing consistently across decades. Optimization on the easy part is rarely the highest-leverage thing the investor can do. The investor who spends ten minutes choosing a reasonable fund and then thirty years contributing to it will outperform the one who spends ten hours choosing the optimal fund and then quits contributing in year three.

What every reader can do this month

If a reader takes nothing else from this book and acts on nothing else, the single most valuable concrete step they can take this month is to set up an automatic monthly contribution to a low-cost broad-market index fund inside a tax-advantaged retirement account. The amount can be small. The point is to start the habit. Once started and automated, the habit runs without further attention, and the compounding does its work in the background while the reader gets on with their life.

This is the action most readers will not take, despite reading every chapter of this book. The reasons are predictable: paperwork feels tedious, the right amount feels uncertain, the right fund feels difficult to choose. None of these reasons survive the slightest examination. The paperwork takes one evening. The amount can be increased later. The fund choice does not have to be optimal — any reasonable broad-market index fund from a major provider works. The reader who completes this single action joins the population that, on the data, ends up with substantially better long-run financial outcomes than the population that does not. The single decision is small. The cumulative effect is enormous.

The boring portfolio, held for thirty years, beats the exciting one almost every time. Time is the active ingredient.

Chapter 28

Wrap up

If you have read this far, the case has been made several times in different forms. This final chapter is a short restatement and a list of practical next steps.

The case in one paragraph

Day trading is a high-cost, high-stress, high-leverage activity in which the structural odds favor the participant's counterparties: market makers, high-frequency firms, brokers earning on activity, course-sellers earning on aspiration, and platforms designed to maximize engagement rather than outcomes. The empirical record across markets and decades shows that the large majority of retail participants lose money over multi-year horizons, and that even disciplined participants face risk of ruin that scales non-linearly with leverage and per-trade size. Long-term investing in productive assets, by contrast, is paid by the underlying economic growth of the businesses owned. It requires far less time and emotional energy and has accumulated decades of evidence supporting its effectiveness for non-professional investors who use low-cost diversified funds, automate contributions, and stay the course.

What to do this week

- If you are not currently day trading and were considering starting: do not start. Read the cited regulator pages from the SEC and FINRA before making any decision.
- If you are currently day trading: track every trade for the next month. Compute realized expectancy after costs. Take the result seriously.
- Open or fund a tax-advantaged retirement account if you have not already. Set up automatic contributions, even at

a small amount.

- If you do not have an emergency fund of three to six months of expenses, build it before doing anything else with risk capital.
- If your spouse or partner does not know the full extent of your trading, schedule the conversation this week.
- If reading this book has made you recognize an addictive pattern, contact a mental-health professional or a behavioral-addiction helpline. Free resources exist; the call costs nothing and may matter.

What to do this year

- Read at least one of: Benjamin Graham's *The Intelligent Investor*, John Bogle's writing on index investing, or William Bernstein's *The Four Pillars of Investing*. None will make you rich quickly. All will help you avoid the most common errors.
- Set a long-term asset allocation that matches your time horizon and risk tolerance. Write it down. Review it once a year.
- If you have been actively trading, consider a six-month break. Note carefully what changes — financially, psychologically, in your relationships.
- If you choose to keep trading, do so with money you can afford to lose, sized as a small fraction of household assets, with no leverage, and without funding it from any source connected to retirement, education, or basic security.

What to do across a working life

- Maximize stable income from work. Compounding career capital is one of the most valuable financial moves available.

- Save consistently. The savings rate matters more than the return at most realistic time horizons.
- Hold a diversified, low-cost portfolio. Rebalance occasionally. Do not panic in drawdowns. Do not chase in bull markets.
- Protect against catastrophe with insurance: health, disability, term life if you have dependents, umbrella liability if your assets are meaningful.
- Stay healthy. The longest financial mistake most people make is shortening their own life.
- Stay connected. Wealth is a means; relationships are the end. Trade fewer times. Call your parents.

A final word

This book has been hard on day trading because the data and the math and the structure all justify being hard. None of that hardness is meant personally for any reader. Most people who attempt day trading are intelligent, ambitious, and looking for a path to financial independence in a system that has not made the conventional paths feel adequate. The motive is good. The strategy chosen, on the evidence, is bad. The good motive deserves a strategy that actually works, and that strategy exists, is well documented, and is available to anyone willing to be patient and consistent.

If this book moves any reader from the losing strategy to the working one — even one reader, with one decade still ahead of them — it will have done its job.

If you choose to keep trading

Some readers will finish this book and decide to keep trading. That is a legitimate choice; it is also the choice the data and the structure of this book have not endorsed. If you are going to do it anyway, do it with the protections that previous chapters have laid out. Use only money you can fully afford to lose. Size positions so that the worst plausible session does not change material life plans. Track every trade and compute realized expectancy after costs. Honor your own daily and weekly loss limits with structural enforcement, not willpower. Maintain at least one wholly market-free day per week and one wholly market-free week per quarter. Talk to your partner. Watch for the patterns of substance use, isolation, and behavioral addiction described in this book and treat them as serious clinical signals when they appear. Above all, do not fund the activity from any source connected to retirement, education, family security, or borrowed money. With those protections in place, day trading at a small fraction of household assets can be a hobby some readers can sustain without destroying anything important. Without them, the activity has the structural features of a slow-motion catastrophe.

If you choose to step back

If reading this book is part of the process by which you decide to step back from active short-term speculation, the next steps matter. The transition can be abrupt or gradual; both work, and the right pace depends on circumstances. The transition that fails most reliably is the one that includes a planned "one more time" return to recover specific losses; the comeback trade is, in nearly every case on record, the trade that delays the actual exit.

A cleaner protocol is to close active positions on a defined schedule, transfer remaining capital into low-cost diversified funds, delete the trading apps from the phone and the desktop, and structure the next thirty days so the urge to check has no convenient outlet. Most former active traders who succeed in transitioning describe the first month as the hardest, the third month as the inflection, and the second year as the moment they realize how much of life had been crowded out and how much returned once the activity stepped back.

What the author hopes for the reader

The author of this book has nothing to gain from your choice between continuing to day trade and switching to long-term diversified investing. There is no course to upsell, no signal service to subscribe to, no platform whose revenue depends on your activity. The only outcome the book optimizes for is that you, ten or twenty or thirty years from now, have more financial security, better relationships, better health, and more peace of mind than the alternative path would have produced.

The data, the math, and the structure all converge on the same recommendation. The reader is the one who has to act on it. If even a few readers, after these pages, choose the patient path that quietly works over the exciting one that quietly does not, the writing was worth the time.

The book in three sentences

Day trading is structurally hostile to ordinary people. The data, the math, the markets, the platforms, the human mind, and the household economics all push the same way. The patient alternative — diversified, low-cost, automated, long-term — is well documented, broadly accessible, and almost always better.

What one decade of patient investing produces

Imagine two readers finishing this book today. Reader A starts day trading with ten thousand dollars and continues for ten years. The expected outcome, based on every available study of retail performance, is that the account is worth less than ten thousand dollars at the end, sometimes substantially less. Reader B contributes five hundred dollars a month into a diversified low-cost index fund for the same ten years and never thinks about it. The expected outcome, based on long-run market history, is an account worth roughly eighty to ninety thousand dollars, depending on returns over the period.

Same starting point. Same ten years. Different decisions. The eighty-thousand-dollar gap is not the result of cleverness. It is the result of letting compounding do its work without interfering. The same gap, extended across a thirty-year working life, produces differences measured in hundreds of thousands of dollars or more, between one household and another, even with similar incomes. Most household financial outcomes that look like luck are actually the cumulative result of these small structural choices, made early and sustained.

A note of thanks

Thank you for reading this far. Books on financial topics rarely get finished, and the fact that you are still here suggests something — that the topic matters to you, that you are thinking honestly about your own situation, that you are willing to consider an unfashionable answer. Whatever you do next with what you have read, that willingness is the trait that produces good outcomes over time. The reader who stays curious, asks honest questions, and adjusts their behavior on evidence rather than enthusiasm tends to end up well, in markets as in everything else.

A final thought on time

The most undervalued asset in this entire book is time. Not market time. Personal time. The hours of a day, the days of a year, the years of a life. Day trading consumes them in volume, often with little to show for it beyond a depleted account and a tired mind. Patient investing returns them. The time freed up by automating financial decisions is time available for work that pays, for family that loves you, for friends who matter, for the body that is the only one you get.

If this book makes any case at all, it is the case for protecting your time. Money is part of how time gets organized; it is not what time is for. The patient path is recommended in these pages partly because it works financially, but also because it leaves you with most of your hours. The activity it replaces takes those hours and gives little back. That trade — hours for outcomes that did not arrive — is the worst trade most readers will ever consider. The best trade is to refuse it, and to spend the time on something that compounds in ways money cannot.

What the patient path leaves you with

Walk forward thirty years from today on the patient path. The reader who automated contributions, owned diversified low-cost index funds, kept a steady job, lived modestly relative to their income, and stayed mostly out of their own way is now in their late fifties or early sixties. Their retirement balance is meaningful — often more than seven figures, depending on income and contribution rate. Their health, on average, is better than the high-stress alternative would have produced. Their relationships, on average, are intact. Their career, on average, advanced steadily through the years they did not spend staring at price charts.

None of this required cleverness. None of it required predicting markets. None of it required watching screens all day. It required the boring decisions, made early and sustained. The reader who ends up at this far point looks back and rarely regrets the boring path. They sometimes regret not starting it earlier. They sometimes regret the years spent on the alternative before they switched. What they almost never regret is the patience itself. The patience is what produced the outcome, and the outcome is what they are living in now.

If this book moves you toward that path — even by a small amount, even if you also decide to keep some small experimental account on the side — the writing was worth the time. The future you, decades from now, will know whether the decision you make this week mattered. Most decisions do not turn out to matter much. This one usually does.

If you read only one chapter again

If a reader will only revisit one chapter of this book in the years ahead, the one to revisit is the chapter on better and safer alternatives. That chapter contains the practical plan that most other chapters point toward. The first edition's warnings, the math of leverage and risk, the human costs of addiction and isolation, the failures of bots and signals — all of these argue against an activity that, on the data, does not work for ordinary people. The alternatives chapter argues for the activity that does.

If the alternatives chapter sticks, the rest of the book has done its job, even if the rest is forgotten. The reader who automates contributions to a low-cost diversified portfolio, builds an emergency fund, pays off high-interest debt, takes care of their career, and protects their relationships and health is on the path that quietly works for most people. They do not need to remember why day trading is hard. They are not doing it. They are doing the thing that, across decades, produces the financial outcome they were looking for. The point of this book is to get them onto that path. The chapter that describes the path is worth keeping close.

Closing words

Thank you for staying with the book to the end. The argument has been made; the practical steps have been outlined; the choice now belongs to the reader. Whatever you do next, do it with full information. The future you, looking back from a calmer distance, will thank the present you for the clarity, even if the clarity was uncomfortable at the time.

> *The path that worked for Graham, Buffett, and millions of quiet long-term investors is still open. It is unglamorous, slow, and reliable. That is the deal.*

www.ingramcontent.com/pod-product-compliance
Lightning Source LLC
LaVergne TN
LVHW100525110826
845146LV00002B/779
* 9 7 9 8 8 9 9 6 5 2 2 4 0 *